Three Cornerstones of Good Governance in the Government

Moral Qualities, the Reliable Pillars of Good Governance

Stephen Mathiang

A Note from the Publisher

The publisher wishes to acknowledge and thank Dr Douglas H. Johnson for his invaluable help and support for Africa World Books and its mission of preserving and promoting African cultural and literary traditions and history. Dr Johnson and fellow historians have been instrumental in ensuring that African people remain connected to their past and their identity. Africa World Books is proud to carry on this mission.

Cover design, typesetting and layout : Africa World Books

Contents

Dedication v

Acknowledgement vii

Preface ix

General Introduction xvii

PART ONE

The Significance of Good Governance in the Executive

Introduction xvii

Chapter 1

Moral Purity in the Executive 1

    Holiness 3

    Righteousness 13

    Justice 22

Chapter 2

Integrity in the Executive 31

    Genuineness 32

    Veracity 40

    Faithfulness 48

Chapter 3

Love in the Executive 57

    Benevolence 60

    Grace 68

    Mercy 75

    Persistence 81

    Summary 88

PART TWO

The Vitality of the Good Governance in the Legislature

Introduction 91

Chapter 4

Moral Purity in the Legislature 95

    Holiness 96

Righteousness 106

Justice 114

Chapter 5

Integrity in the Legislature 125

Genuineness 126

Veracity 134

Faithfulness 142

Chapter 6

Love in the Legislature 153

Benevolence 154

Grace 166

Mercy 176

Persistence 186

Summary 195

PART THREE

The Importance of Good Governance in Judiciary

Introduction 199

Chapter 7

Moral Purity in the Judiciary 203

Holiness 206

Righteousness 208

Justice 211

Chapter 8

Integrity in the Judiciary 215

Genuineness 216

Veracity 219

Faithfulness 221

Chapter 9

Love in the Judiciary 225

Benevolence 226

Grace 232

Mercy 234

Persistence 236

Summary 238

General Conclusion 239

Exercises 242

Bibiography 243

Dedication

It is fully dedicated to all the past, the present and the future global advocates for good moral values and good governance. Above all, it is dedicated to all lovers of our moral God, the only reliable source of good moral qualities.

Acknowledgements

L oners never excel in life. Therefore, I thank friends and relatives who appreciate my knowledge and creativity and hence, encouraged me to write this book on leadership that seeks to contribute solutions on leadership and moral issues in today's world.

I highly appreciate the relentless support given to me by my loving wife Elizabeth Agot Leek in the course of my writing. This is the very purpose for which God brought us together: to help each other as we go up and down in life. My children, Ajoh, Kuch, Alier, Jogaak, Areu and my nephew Kuch Bech have also been of much help to me. May the Lord make them His unwavering followers and help them excel in life even more than I! I love all of you.

Last, but not the least, I am very grateful to my good editor Wilson N. Macharia who used his professionalism to make this book an interesting read.

Preface

The fact that people are crying for good governance in the government and other organizations is a clear indication that good governance is generally lacking, even though in principle it is provided for in constitutions. There is a wide gap between what many governments and other agencies in the world promise the citizens and what they deliver. This book seeks to address the mounting cry for good governance. I am aware there are many books on this subject and others are still being published. But I intend to move the reader from the realm of superficial solutions to the root cause of the problem and hence, the real solution.

Today, marks of poor governance, such as injustice and corruption are pervasive and widespread. Lack of good moral values is the main culprit when it comes to poor governance in both private and public establishments.

Moreover, in writing this book, it is appreciated that poor governance is sometimes the result of lack of knowledge of the constitutional mandate and how key arms of government relate to each other rather than lack of political will. I have therefore, devoted a considerable section of the book to explain the mandate of each of the arms of government and how the three relate.

Moral deficiencies are the ones that have bedevilled peace in most parts of the world for decades. Therefore, what the times cry for are virtues such as moral purity, integrity and love for others if we are to promote good governance in any given community. Where there is purity, righteousness and justice, the rights of individuals are cherished. Also the defining features of integrity and love are important ingredients of good governance.

On the other hand, the results of bad moral values are evil thoughts, murder, adultery, sexual immorality, theft, false testimony, slander, impurity, hatred, discord, jealousy, selfish ambition, dissensions, faction, envy and drunkenness. Unfortunately, these common vices that undermine productivity and cohesion in society are the ones that make the media appeal to the general public and become such a lucrative business, as they make for catchy, tantalizing headlines in the newspapers, radio and TV.

Numerous attempts have been made in different parts of the world to find the root cause of poor governance and deal with it. Not long ago, capitalism was touted as the system that would be the panacea for the socio-economic and political problems. Capitalism is that economic system that promotes private ownership of the means of production and distribution. It protects the freedom of capitalists to operate and manage their property for profit in a competitive environment.

But capitalism has proven to have its downside in that it creates a few rich people who end up oppressing and exploiting the majority poor. Although capitalism is currently the most popular economic system in the world, it is common knowledge that good governance cannot flourish where there is oppression and exploitation of man by fellow man.

Communism came up as a promising proletarian system of government to find some lasting solutions to poor governance. Communists advocated for a classless society in which private ownership of property was going to be non-existent and the means of production belonging to the community or government. It promised to deal with injustice and similar vices while at the same time establishing a secular government that stands for equality, progress and unity. This idealistic system that is in direct opposition to capitalism did also fail to bring about good governance. Today, there are still pockets of communism in the world, though the zeal of its proponents has been waning.

Many in the world view democracy as a workable antidote to poor governance. This is a governance system owned and managed by people through their elected representatives. It works as a political and social system that is based on the idea and spirit of social equality. That is why it is viewed as owned by people through their representatives. At the moment, democracy seems to be the star that is shedding light along the path of development, since its principles tend to work well where they are correctly applied.

From the onset, it is important to understand that democracy and capitalism go hand in hand as two sides of the same coin. Unlike communists, supporters of democracy do not see capitalism as oppressive and exploitative. They view it is as fair, since it is driven by profit and market forces, not individual whims. Unfortunately, under this system, the few rich get richer, while the poor majority become poorer. The evidence of the weakness of this oppressive and exploitative system is the presence of sprawling slums that sandwich enclaves of opulence in the metropolitan cities, especially in the Third World. This state of affairs is explained away with the argument that the poor are poor because they are lazy and the rich are rich because they work harder. No doubt one ought to work hard for self-improvement, but is hard work the only way of accumulating resources?

Although capitalism, communism and democracy have made their little contribution towards human development, they have been unable to deliver satisfactory solutions to poor governance. For Good governance is achieved through living by the morality stipulated in God's Word, not pursuing men's ideas. The government and its organs may come up with laws, but that cannot make one do what is right unless they choose to do so. Although a morally deviant person may be afraid of laws and the different regulations of his society, these will not reform him because they do not address the root cause of his moral problem. Rules merely deal with the symptoms of poor moral values. Indeed, jailing or fining a thief alone will not deter him from stealing again. The root cause of his moral problem, and the one that makes him a thief, will need to be dealt with first. Even if such a person does not steal for fear of the harsh penalties, he remains a thief inside so long as his own conscience still favours theft, and it will just be a matter of time before he steals again if he gets an opportunity.

Am I saying that rules are not important in maintaining law and order in society? Not at all! What I am saying is that for human beings to live amicably, they must first identify the root cause of bad behaviour and address it. The core value of leaders of governments who do things that are beneficial to their people is empathising with them. Loving others as you love yourself should be a way of life. Unfortunately, as noted elsewhere in this book, our leaders easily give in to greed and allure of the kind of life that cannot be afforded with mere salary.

But leaders ought to rein in the desire for extravagant lifestyle and strive to live within their means. Moreover, the common people could contribute to the accountability of their leaders by refraining from making remarks that could be misconstrued as vindicating stealing from public coffers to enrich oneself.

At this point, let me mention that human wickedness is from within and not from outside the wicked person. For one to realise a positive change morally, therefore, he must start by dealing with the condition of his heart, since it is from one's heart that comes "evil thoughts, murder, adultery, sexual immorality, theft, false testimony, slander" (Matt. 15:19). These are some of the common results of poor moral values. Although our laws may serve to reduce the gravity of the effects of poor moral values, they can never bring about lasting change to the human heart. No human law can make an immoral person come out of his moral bondage, for the Scriptures says, "Though you grind a fool in a mortar, grinding him like grain with a pestle, you will not remove his folly from him" (Pr. 27:22).

Poor moral values are a reflection of our sinful nature. This outward expression of the character of a person who is estranged from God is sometimes referred to as the carnal mind. God is the ultimate source of moral goodness; therefore, when a person is separated from God, he loses the desire for good moral values and instead pursues the acts of the flesh or sinful nature. According to Apostle Paul, "The acts of the sinful nature are obvious: sexual immorality, impurity and debauchery; idolatry and witchcraft; hatred, discord, jealousy, fits of rage, selfish ambition, dissensions, factions and envy; drunkenness, orgies, and the like" (Gal. 5:19-21). Human laws may restrain the full expression of these and other common vices, but they will not satisfactorily address them because human laws merely control behaviour of people but do not change the heart. If not dealt with from the root, these overt acts of sinful nature tend to paralyse man morally and negatively affect governance. The result of this is chaos that we are all too familiar with.

Since this sinful nature is the result of man's separation from God, we can only deal with it through seeking reconciliation with Him, based on His terms, of course. If we seek God diligently, we will find Him and He will come into our lives and live with us. God in us means the presence of His Spirit in us. And when we maintain friendship with Him, He will enable us to manifest the fruit of the Spirit in our daily life. The acts of sinful nature are contrary to those of the fruit of the Spirit. In the Bible it is written: "But the fruit of the Spirit is love, joy, peace, patience, kindness, goodness, faithfulness, gentleness and self-control… Those who belong to Christ Jesus have crucified the sinful nature with its passions and desires" (Gal. 5:22). The fruit of the Spirit promotes peace and is lifesaving. Good governance exists where people's lives are characterized by the fruit of the Spirit.

Having become familiar with the fruit of the sinful nature and that of the Spirit, it is now up to us to make a choice. People can choose either enmity with God and reap the results of the sinful nature that lead to poor governance or do the will of God and reap the fruit of the Spirit which results in good governance.

Personally, in my attempt to investigate and establish enduring solutions to man's problems, I found out that man without God is inherently sinful. His sinful nature started at the Fall of Adam and Eve in the Garden of Eden. As a result, God's image in man was marred by the works of the devil. Since the Fall, Satan has been constantly enticing man to continue committing sin.

Ever since man was chased out of Eden, there has been a constant spiritual war over him between God, the Creator, and Satan, the distorter and liar. God has always wanted to forgive and restore man to his original state and equip him fully with godly moral qualities. This is why He sent Jesus Christ to the world to come and die for mankind; indeed, Jesus said, "I have come that they may have life, and have it to the full" (Jn. 10:10b). This, in a nutshell, is the mission statement of Jesus Christ. And the life He refers to is one without moral corruption, a life full of good deeds, honesty and pure thoughts, a life that is impossible to realize until one has placed their faith in Jesus Christ.

Satan's mission statement, on the other hand, is revealed in John 10:10 where the Bible says in part: "The thief comes only to steal and kill and destroy". Indeed, since the fall of man at the Garden of Eden, life on earth has been characterized by stealing, killing and all manner of destruction, fulfilling Satan's manifesto to the letter.

But man has the option to turn to God for the solution to his problems. I am a witness that man can fully repent and turn to God, his Creator, and from there on have a meaningful life and have it more abundantly. This book is intended to help you do just that, and also show you how the results of the new life—moral purity, integrity and love—can be used as the three cornerstones of good governance. It is my hope that reading it will make you join hands with the other peace-loving and morally upright people in their zealous quest for good governance.

Stephen Mathiang

General Introduction

People, particularly those who are coming from a war of independence, regard freedom of managing their own affairs with a lot of hope. But in most cases, having a constitution, a flag and indigenous people in positions of authority does not translate into good governance, a prerequisite for social harmony and prosperity.

Having public money at your disposal, especially at the initial stages of nationhood before checks and balances for managing government resources have been developed, brings with it the temptation of putting part of it to personal use. Over time, government officers acquire an extravagant lifestyle that mere salary cannot bankroll. Years later, such lifestyle and argument of justifying it to advance become widespread among government workers. Even euphemisms for such kind of theft are invented to sooth the conscience of those involved in it. That is how corruption becomes embedded in society. This situation is compounded by elders who see nothing wrong with one of their own sons siphoning money from the amorphous entity called government to enrich himself and earn their clan respectability.

Many nations, especially in Africa, have become hostage to greedy leaders who have no qualms stuffing their accounts with money obtained by dubious means. But the negative social effects of misdirecting public funds are many. These include inability to give services that only the government is responsible for giving—like good roads—and shrinking economies and the social crises that go with them, like joblessness, high cost of living and insecurity. Although you may come up with all manner of ways to sweep the concerns of the travailing masses under the carpet while you enrich yourself, at some point these disenfranchised people will look for ways to bring their plight to the attention of the public, be it through unedifying spectacles like demonstrations.

Sadly, a poll carried out recently in a leading university in East Africa revealed that most of the students see nothing wrong with getting involved in scams to siphon money from the Exchequer to individual accounts to facilitate flashy lifestyles. To them, the end justifies the means. And with prospective government workers reasoning that way, it is clear that corruption and the social challenges that go with it are with us for the long haul unless there is deliberate effort to show the right way of doing things and change poisonous ways of thinking. We have the responsibility of instilling godly values into the next generation so that they become acquainted with the principles that will bring peace and prosperity to their nations.

A good government starts to work when leaders rein in their selfish desires and start doing things for the common good of the nation as a whole. If our nations are to remain sovereign and respected by the global community, their governments must operate in a way that will bring about social harmony and development among their people. And there can be no peace when resources that are supposed to serve the interests of many are being squandered by a few at the top. If the nation is experiencing prosperity, the benefits of that prosperity should reach everybody.

Moral qualities are the reliable pillars of good governance in any society. By moral qualities I mean all aspects of moral purity, integrity and love. God created man in His image and likeness (Gen. 1:26-27), endowing him with some of His moral attributes such as goodness to enable him rule fairly over the earth.

Before the fall of man in the Garden of Eden, the earth was full of God's glory (Gen. 2:9), with man enjoying intimacy with his own Creator. Actually, God took all other creatures to him to name them, and man did it (Gen. 2:19-20a). Therefore, one can conclude here that what took place in the Garden of Eden prior to the entry of sin was the best model of governance because that time man was entirely controlled by morality.

However, Satan was not happy with this cordial and harmonious relationship between God and mankind. So, he enticed both Adam and Eve to disobey their Creator. Regrettably, they fell into Satan's trick by disobeying God's command and eating the fruit of the forbidden tree (Gen. 3:6). They thought eating the fruit of this tree would make them wiser like God, but, instead, God expelled this poor couple from the Garden of Eden. Because of their isolation from the goodness of God, Adam and Eve became morally corrupt, and they passed on this sinful nature to their descendants. This inherited sin led to the murder of Abel by his rude brother Cain (Gen. 4:8). Ever since, mankind has suffered from lack of good moral values as evident from poor governance and destructive behaviour by people.

By pursuing immoral values, man has subjected the entire world to untold suffering and destruction. Indeed, people killing and oppressing others is a fact that is all too familiar. People also make life hard for other creatures on the earth. At some point God became unbearably grieved by the sinfulness of man as evident in Gen. 6:5: "The Lord saw how great man's wickedness on the earth had become, and that every inclination of the thoughts of his heart was only evil all the time". Because of this moral decay, God reached the following sad conclusion in verse 7: … "I will wipe mankind, whom I have created, from the face of the earth—men and animals, and creatures that move along the ground, and birds of the air - for I am grieved that I have made them." Sin is very, very contagious!

Due to pervasiveness and ubiquity of sin, God destroyed the whole world through the flood except Noah and his family members and other creatures selected by species and gender to re-inhabit the earth. God saved Noah because he (Noah) had found favour in his eyes (Gen. 6:8). Noah's life shows us that despite the rampant wickedness of one's day, one can choose to be different and be after God's own heart and make a difference for God in a depraved society. Such are the godly men and women who persistently strive to create a conducive atmosphere for good governance in all sectors of human life!

In spite of the near-annihilation of all living creatures by God at the time of Noah, the descendants of Noah clearly did not learn a lesson. Instead, they perpetuated the wickedness of their forefathers. Once again God was grieved and in Genesis 19, we see the total destruction of Sodom and Gomorrah.

But in order for God to restore man to his original relationship with his Creator, He had been carrying out a long-term plan and at some point called Abram as a key person in fulfilling it, saying, 'I will make you into a great nation and I will bless you; I will make your name great, and you will be a blessing. I will bless those who bless you, and whoever curses you I will curse; and all peoples on earth will be blessed through you' (Gen. 12:2-3). This divine covenant between God and Abraham was part of God's effort to bring into the world the Seed of the woman that was to crush Satan's head (Gen. 3:15). Christ, the seed of the woman according to Galatians 4:4, eventually came to the earth through Abraham's lineage. Despite God's covenant with Abraham, wickedness among human beings and the attendant sufferings on the earth kept increasing. This is evidenced by the great loss of life that kept recurring and destruction of other innocent creatures and beautiful landscapes in the hands of ungodly people and harsh nature.

Man was still grappling with the undesirable results of sin by the time Jesus Christ was born. Poor governance was widespread in the world due to immoral values or sinful nature. Indeed, Christ came to preach good news to the poor, to proclaim freedom to the prisoners, recovery of sight for the blind, to release the oppressed and to proclaim the year of the Lord's favour (Lk. 4:18-19). He actually came to reconcile man to his Creator (Rom. 5:11; 2 Cor. 5:18-19). He came to free man from his sinful nature and restore him to his original state in God's kingdom.

But this message of reconciliation only benefits the person who genuinely and faithfully responds to it by accepting Jesus Christ as his or her Lord and Saviour. It is only after this spiritual change, and hence reunion with the Father, that a person is able to reclaim his moral qualities and starts discharging his divine duties as required in Gen. 1:26.

It is now more than two thousand years since Christ came to earth to bring the Good News. But the world is still experiencing moral corruption and lack of good governance in different areas of life, including the church. Hence, the question: Can a person who has been reconciled to God through Jesus Christ contribute to good governance on earth? The purpose of this book is to highlight the key elements of good governance in the light of God's moral qualities, and by so doing show the correct answer to the above question. Since human beings in their depraved condition are incapable of bringing about "better" or the "best" governance, this book challenges them to reclaim their good moral values, and good governance will follow.

Nevertheless, we must understand from the outset that being a Christians does not make us morally upright effortlessly; one must genuinely abandon their sins and offer oneself as a living sacrifice to God, submitting oneself to the control of Christ through the power of His Holy Spirit.

The Government cannot be corrupt if its workers are not corrupt, but it will be ethically corrupt if the people manning it suffer from moral deficiency. Good governance is only possible when workers are constantly testing their behaviour against the magnifying lenses of God's moral attributes and making it conform to the requirements in God's Word. God's moral attributes are the leadership guide in the kingdom of God. By God's moral attributes I mean the characteristics of God, the ultimate moral Being. The word "corruption" has its origin in people's immoral attributes. Where there are no ethical values, there can be no good governance.

The focus of this book is to explore how moral purity (holiness, righteousness and justice), integrity (genuineness, veracity and faithfulness) and love (benevolence, grace, mercy and persistence) can enhance good governance in the main arms of government—the executive, the legislature and the judiciary. In other books which I am in the process of writing, I have also shown how moral qualities are capable of bringing good governance in the church and family. I recommend you read them too so as to be more familiar with the different ways by which good governance can benefit mankind.

Although this book draws heavily from the teahings in the Bible in addressing the problems of governance, almost every religion seeks to fight immorality because its negative effect on mankind affects everybody. Before you reach the end of the book, you are sure to have realized that morality is a critical pillar of good governance.

The arms of government

Many countries have three main arms of government—the executive, the legislature, and the judiciary. This is in keeping with separation of powers, a management principle. This separation brings bout accountability by ensuring that the powers of the government are not concentrated in the hands of any single person or set of persons. The three arms are:

- the Executive
- the Legislature
- the Judiciary

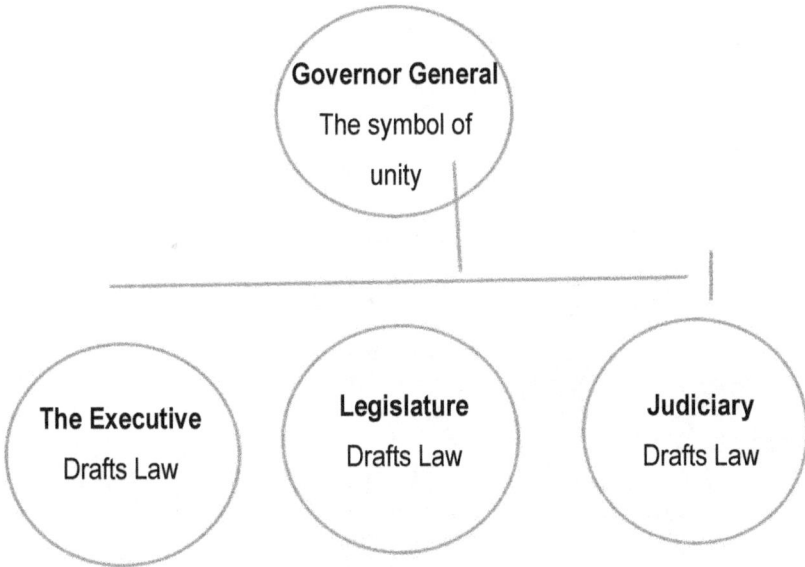

Governor General
The symbol of
unity

The Executive
Drafts Law

Legislature
Drafts Law

Judiciary
Drafts Law

PART ONE – THE EXECUTIVE
The Importance of Good Governance in the Executive

CHAPTER 1
Moral Purity in the Executive

CHAPTER 2
Integrity in the Executive

CHAPTER 3
Love in the Executive

Introduction

The Executive

Consists of president or prime minister, governor, Cabinet ministers and government departments

The executive is headed by the president or prime minister or governor, depending on the structure and levels of the government. The executive proposes policy, drafts bills, and implements the policy that has been enacted and funded by the legislative branch through government departments. Also, the executive is in charge of the armed forces and represents the state in international pacts, etc.

When the executive branch adheres to its mandate, good governance is realized in all areas of the government. Starting from the office of the president down to the different government ministries and departments, things should be guided by good moral values. This way, the executive will relate well with the legislature and judiciary in discharging their obligations. As a result, the citizens enjoy political, economic, social and other forms of prosperity. Under such circumstances, people working in the executive are good civil servants, doing whatever they do, not only to realize personal goals but also to meet national aspirations. Policies on foreign affairs are also well planned and implemented without compromising national interests. Good governance is realized and improved with the passage of time, as everything done is based on sound ethical values.

When the executive branch proposes public policy, drafts bills, implements and monitors public policy, commands all armed forces and acts as state's representative, among other responsibilities, with the wrong motive, the nation begins to lose its focus. The result is poor coordination and cooperation between the executive, legislature and judiciary, as they cease to carry out their separate duties on the basis of mutual trust. If this trend is not stopped early enough, it will lead to undesirable results, namely: 1) the emerging of unhealthy groupings within the executive, with patriotic people clashing with the selfish ones, 2) the erosion of harmonious relationship between the executive, legislature and judiciary, 3) poor governance becomes a common feature of the executive, in particular, and the entire government in general, and 4) people begin to lose faith in their leader and those who work with him in the executive and, subsequently, the entire government. They see them as selfish people who are in power to cause confusion and meet their egocentric desires. This gives the nation a bad image in the eyes of its citizens as well as in the eyes of international community. In such circumstances, the common response among citizens is the desire to quit the government at once and look for their better replacements.

Normally, the consequences of poor governance include civil strife that has been common in different parts of the world. Today, civil conflicts are common in many places in Africa, Europe, Asia, and Middle East, among other places. And the reason is because of the civil servants failing, to a certain extent, to be guided by good moral values in their actions and character.

Part One of this book seeks to prove the importance of good governance in the executive if there is to be good governance in the government. For clarity in addressing the topic, I have divided the executive into chief executive or president, the cabinet (comprising the ministers and their deputies) and the bureaucrats, including the armed forces.

Chapter One explores how these top government officers can promote good governance by having their conduct, their relationship and the way they discharge their national duties informed by moral purity — holiness, righteousness and justice. Chapter Two will do the same in respect of aspects of moral integrity, that is, genuineness, veracity and faithfulness. Chapter Three will examine good governance in light of the four characteristics of the divine love, which are benevolence, grace, mercy and persistence.

Chapter 1
Moral Purity in the Executive

Compromised Executive

A mong other responsibilities, the executive is mandated to appoint heads of key government departments and parastatals. These people are put in charge of vast government resources and manage government expenditure that involves paying out huge sums of money. With this awareness, corrupt executives have been appointing people to these important positions, not on the basis of their honesty and vision for improving the economy but because they are easy to bend to their whims and will be easy to compromise when it becomes necessary to plunder government coffers for the benefit of the executive. One way of doing this is through awarding huge government contracts to shadowy individuals and people who deliberately overcharge with the connivance of government appointed officers and their cut in the deal banked abroad so as not to raise eyebrows. This money is then used to buy the executives and their yes men mansions abroad and for educating their children in distant lands.

Importance of Moral Purity in the Executive

In order to see the importance of moral purity in our daily lives, let us consider definitions of the frightening word, "corruption". According to E. Nwabuzor, M. Mueller, and M. McMullen, "a public official is corrupt if he accepts money or money's worth for doing something that he is under a duty to do anyway, that he is under a duty not to do, or to exercise a legitimate discretion for improper reasons."[1]

Going by this brief definition, corruption in the government in Africa is the order of the day and is of very high magnitude. Government officials are usually strongly suspected of or implicated in corruption. The police, too, are known to receive bribes. In many countries, the judiciary is a haven of corruption. Over time, this vice has permeated into the corporate sector as well. This is despite the fact that "The promise of almost every new ruler – whether military or civilian – is to stamp out corruption. So far their success has been light."[2]

God is the source of moral purity, an indication of His total separation from anything wicked or evil. He is the ultimate standard when it comes to doing well; whatever He does is right. So if we were to align our actions to God's plan and have them guided by God's moral purity, the result would be goodness. When government officials are morally corrupt, we would be asking for the impossible to expect good governance from them; after all, people reap what they sow. That is the rule of nature that is corroborated even by God's Word. Consider the following words of Jesus in the holy Bible:

> Watch out for false prophets. They come to you in sheep's clothing, but inwardly they are ferocious wolves.

---

1 E. Nwabuzor and M. Mueller, An Introduction to Political Science for African Students, (The Macmillan Ltd: Hong Kong, 1985), 135.
2 Ibid., Mueller, 135.

By their fruit you will recognize them. Do people pick grapes from thorn bushes, or figs from thistles? Likewise every good tree bears good fruit, but a bad tree bears bad fruit. A good tree cannot bear bad fruit, and a bad tree cannot bear good fruit (Matt. 7:15-18).

In order for us to realise good governance in the executive, all the officials, starting from the top leadership, must embrace God's moral purity in their own lives as they carry out their national duties. If their behaviour is morally right, they will automatically do good work, but if they are morally corrupt, the results of their actions will be bad just the way a bad tree will not bear good fruit.

Let us now see how good governance in the executive should be guided by God's moral purity that is characterized by holiness, righteousness and justice.

Holiness

'Who among the gods is like you, O Lord? Who is like you — majestic in holiness, awesome in glory, working wonders?' This is the Lord who governs his universe in the light of his holiness, making it the abode of the good governance. He is also the One who gives those who live in this world the ability to exercise good governance if they happen to invite him into their own lives. God expects us to use His holiness as a yardstick for the evaluation of good governance in the executive. It is only through divine holiness that good governance can be fully realised.

The discussion here will focus on the president, the cabinet plus all other such parties, like armed forces. Let's consider ways in which holiness can influence good governance in the area of the presidency. Of course one of the common, but naïve, questions in the minds of some of my readers is whether a person could attain God's holiness in their life. But just hold your breath and let's see how the president could realise this task that seems hard to some, since all things are possible in the Lord.

Importance of the Holiness of a President

When a president strives to lead the nation in holiness, God is happy with him and begins to work through him, showering the nation with His blessings. Of course a human being cannot achieve holiness without the help of a holy God, for God is the true source of holiness. Really, one's holiness is an indication of his union with the Lord and hence separation from Satan and all his evil forces.

A holy president diligently avoids all manner of Satanic influences and sinful acts like sexual immorality, impurity and debauchery, idolatry and witchcraft, hatred, discord, jealousy, fits of rage, selfish ambition, dissensions, factions and envy, drunkenness, orgies, and the like (Gal. 5:19-21). As a result, the holy Lord rewards this effort by helping the president embrace and internalise the fruit of the Spirit, that is, love, joy, peace, patience, kindness, goodness, faithfulness, gentleness and self-control (Gal. 5:22-23) and all other desirable moral attributes. Such a head of state serves and leads his people in line with God's will. Under his leadership, the nation enjoys peace, unity and prosperity. He also impacts his followers and others with the essence of divine holiness, becoming the torchbearer of ethical norms and good governance in and outside the national boundaries. Such is the kind of admirable leader who verbally advocates for a peaceful world in which human rights and moral values are cherished and safeguarded.

But when a president disregards holiness, the holy Lord also disregards him because God does not delight in moral impurity. Henceforth, such a president's life gets under the direct control and influence of Satan and his evil forces. As a result, he loses the sense of good moral character. Such a leader is unable to see things from God's perspective, viewing them, instead, through the eyes of Satan. He embraces moral impurity instead of moral purity. As an individual, he indulges in all kinds of immoralities at the expense of his wife and children, setting a bad picture to the nation.

Instead of attracting God's blessings upon himself, his family and the entire nation, he angers the Lord and causes Him to pour His wrath upon the land. Before long, the nation is engulfed by socio-economic and political turmoil. Such are the poor global leaders who guide their nations and the whole world along the path of darkness at the end of which is imminent doom. Few such leaders die in their homeland, and even if they die at home, their end is characterized by ignominy.

But what is the biblical view of good leadership? James D. Berkley defines it as follows:

> Biblical leadership takes place when divinely appointed men and women respond in obedience to God's call. They recognise the importance of preparation time, allowing the Holy Spirit to develop tenderness of heart and skill of hands. They carry out their leadership roles with a deep conviction of God's will and an acute awareness of the contemporary issues they and their followers face. Above all, they exercise leadership as servants and stewards, sharing authority with their followers and affirming that leadership is primarily ministry to others, modelling for others, and mutual membership with others in Christ's body.[3]

This means that a leader should understand that he has a

---

3   Leadership Handbook of Management and Administration: Practical insight from a cross section of ministry leaders, ed. James D. Berkley (Grand Rapids, Michigan: Baker Books, 1994), 147.

divine duty to lead His people at the time he comes to power. Of course there have been, and still are, some self-imposed leaders worldwide, but only God knows how to deal with them. I have no intention to discuss such in this book.

A leader who is divinely appointed by the Lord should allow God's Holy Spirit to guide his heart and his hands. That way, he will be prepared to love and lead his people in accordance with God's will. Moreover, he should exercise his leadership role as a servant and steward, involving those under him in governance, thus affirming that leadership is primarily about serving others. Leadership is also about mentoring others and playing your role in the body of Christ.

As a leader, do you really know who placed you where you are and what those under you expect of you? Well, as you ponder on this question, let me tell you that the Lord expects the state president to work towards emulating Him. The leader should make God the standard against which to fashion his moral character, irrespective of the president's religious background. The entire moral code emanates from God, the source of goodness. He told the Children of Israel, "I am the Lord your God; consecrate yourselves and be holy, because I am holy. Do not make yourselves unclean by any creature that moves about on the ground...therefore be holy, because I am holy" (Lev. 11: 44-45).

Every president should consecrate (set apart) himself for God's work. He should live a righteous life before God, for the Lord is holy. And for the leader to be able to live a holy life, he must allow the holy God to have unrestricted control of his personal life. That is, he is to make God the Lord of his life by abiding in Him and operating through Him on a daily basis so that the leader's words become God's words, his actions God's actions and his thoughts God's thoughts. This is called daily communion with God. Such a leader should avoid defiling himself by involving himself in corruption, since doing so is against God's will. Like God, the president should not only be free from moral wickedness but should also refuse to tolerate the presence of evil in his own government.

The office of the president should also be made an abode for God by separating it from unclean things. In order for the president to see the necessity for a complete overhaul of his moral and spiritual condition, he should not regard himself or other people as the standard of holiness; he should evaluate his holiness by using God's holiness as the standard.

The reason I emphasize the importance of holiness in the personal life of the national president is because he is God's appointee to be the torchbearer for good governance in his state. He has the executive powers to instil good moral values in the lives of the people in and beyond the government circle. He is the primary teacher of good moral values, God's spokesman in disseminating the godly principles of leadership and ethical behaviour among the people for the common good of mankind and for God's own glory.

It is vital to emphasize here that God qualifies to teach people to be holy because He Himself is holy. Needless to say, He cannot teach what He is not a part of. In the same way, for a good preacher to deliver a life-changing sermon from the church pulpit, he must first have saturated his entire life with that message, with the help of the Holy Spirit of course. You cannot give what you do not have; you cannot persuasively teach what is not a part of you. It is quite important, therefore, for the state president, unless God has not called him to the position of his leadership, to seek to emulate God in holiness so as to be in a position to teach others to be holy, too. This is a biblical requirement that must always be satisfied.

When the nation has a holy president, the possibility of good governance is very high because such a leader will influence his staff to make decisions affecting the state in light of God's holiness. With this awareness, the public should beseech God to give them holy leaders, those who are God-fearing and whom God has put aside to guide His people.

It is the duty of the electorates to put in that position a person of high moral values, one who wears God's holiness as his invisible attire on daily basis as he leads the nation along the path of moral goodness. National leadership positions should go to people of unquestionable character.

Effect of Holiness in the Cabinet

In order for the president to be a capable torchbearer, he should have the solid backing of a God-fearing cabinet. Let us now consider how a godly cabinet, one that promotes good governance, should be.

When members of the cabinet fashion their individual behaviour and social relationships after God's Word, they act collectively and individually as reliable pillars of the president. This is because the success or failure of any human leader is dependent on those around him, especially his subordinates. A cabinet that fears the Lord has daily communion with Him, and this makes it possible for it to deliberate on and come up with considerate (and hence, effective) policies on governance. Such a cabinet assists the president in upholding and promoting good moral values in the executive, thus, leading in the effort towards good governance. Their holiness repels all acts of sin and all known vices targeted at the executive arm of the government. They speak against corruption with authority through their actions because they are not involved in the vice. They are actually the torchbearers of good governance within and outside the executive. As a result, even the general public come to love them and appreciate their services.

But when individual members of the cabinet are not yielded

to the Spirit of God, the holy Lord is also absent in their lives. As a result, Satan exploits this opportunity to invade and control their lives, making them his servants instead of being good civil servants. Evil members of the cabinet protect actions that are guided by poor morals, like corruption, and allow themselves to be guided by them in their own behaviour and relationships. And so, even if their president happens to be determined to lead a holy life, their corrupt utterances and actions go counter to the good intentions of their leader. Eventually, their deliberate wickedness attracts God's wrath upon them and upon the whole nation. In fact, the reason some of the nations in the world today are sighing under God's curse is because of the ungodliness of their cabinets.

But what do God and righteous people want of the cabinet members? First of all, the cabinet consists of all government ministers, their deputies and advisors, and it is chaired by the president. They are the key pillars of the executive. Like the president, cabinet members should emulate God's holiness as they discharge their national duties on a day-to-day basis. God expects them to be holy just as He is holy. They are to abstain from any sort of malpractices and, instead, uphold godliness in all that they do. The cabinet must understand that God put them in leadership positions to govern their people according to His will, promoting equal rights and protecting the weak and the poor as well as providing religious freedom.

If members of the cabinet embrace holiness, this will automatically transform the state systems, leading to good governance. But if they pursue unethical behaviour, their government will stand defiled, thus, bringing God's curse upon the nation. This is the way God requires both the president and the cabinet to uphold holiness so as to be able to steer their people towards good governance. When the time of election comes, it is the noble role of the electorates to choose holy people and for the national president and other relevant authorities to choose key people in leadership positions, using moral behaviour and personal relationship to God as criteria for selection. An unholy people defile the cabinet and make it unholy, too.

Let's not fight corruption with mere words within the four corners of executive building or just in the media; after all, even people who work in the press can be corrupted to serve vested interest. With the help of the Holy Spirit, we ought to fight corruption passionately by word and deed. Inanimate objects are not corrupt but human beings are.

But the holiness of both the president and his cabinet members alone cannot bring about good governance if those under them are immoral. Let us now explore the importance of the holiness of lower cadre staff of the executive.

The Importance of the Holiness of Bureaucrats

For the purpose of this book, 'bureaucrats' refers to the administrative body of appointed officials within the executive arm of the government. These are men and women appointed as government officials to carry out its administrative tasks. They handle enormous amount of work routinely. The fact of the matter is that for any government to execute a major national project, having an efficient and clearly structured bureaucracy is one of the prerequisites.

If the bureaucrats base their moral values and personal dealings on God's holiness, they will surely attract God's backing because holiness will make them living abodes of the holy Lord. At the same time, their intimate relationship with God will compel them avoid poor moral values and any type of satanic influences and, instead, subordinate their personal interests under the national interests. Their holiness will help them execute their administrative tasks and other national duties for the common good of the nation. They see people the way God sees them — as people, not trees — irrespective of their geographic location, ethnicity, religious, economic and political affiliation. As a result, the holy God makes them successful in all their endeavours. They are the reliable and successful pillars of their cabinet and, by extension, the president. Such bureaucrats are strong promoters of good governance.

When bureaucrats lack holiness, this does not go well for the nation. First of all, since they lack the holiness of God, God's presence is not in their lives. In its place is satanic spirit to guide them in doing evil. Due to satanic influence, such bureaucrats do not bear the fruit of the Spirit in their lives. They portray, instead, acts of sinful nature, thus, discharging their administrative activities in an ungodly manner by putting their individual interests above the national interests. To facilitate corruption, unholy bureaucrats promote division among the citizens and between them and the government, thus, letting down the cabinet and the president. Given their large number and hence, the effect of their actions, unholy bureaucrats can easily bring down their nation to its knees. At some point, their immoral actions draw God's wrath on them and the whole nation.

But what does God want of the bureaucrats? God expects the bureaucrats to be holy, as He, too, is holy. God wants them to emulate His holiness, the ultimate standard of moral character; after all, the whole moral code is based on His holiness. They should always be guided by such holiness as they carry out their national tasks. Their words, deeds and thoughts should be guided by God's holiness because whatever slight mistakes they make could attract God's wrath and bring down the nation to its knees.

The holiness of the president and his cabinet alone is not enough to attract God's blessings to the nation; the holiness of the entire team of bureaucrats is necessary as well. Every government official is supposed to serve citizens indiscriminately for the national good and also for God's glory. Hence, for good governance to flourish, the bureaucrats, as God's appointees, should separate themselves from unclean things, including corruption, choosing to act righteously instead (2 Cor. 6:14-7:1).

Those who have discovered God's light are aware that there should be no fellowship or compromise with darkness (1 Cor. 10:20-21) when people are seeking the face of God. Separation with the world means more than keeping our distance from sinners; it means staying close to God, who is the ultimate source of holiness. It involves more than avoiding worldly entertainment; it extends to being careful how we spend our time and money, since they too should contribute to realizing God's will.

Civil servants in other branches of government, for example, the armed forces, should also uphold God's holiness, taking God's holiness as the yardstick of their conduct. It is only if the whole executive is guided by God's holiness as it formulates national policies, that there will be God's blessings and prosperity in the land. For there to be good governance that is guided by God's moral purity, the executive must discharge all its national duties in light of God's holiness.

It is part of the national duty of the top leadership in the executive, the legislature and the judiciary to properly screen men and women to hold key positions. These people who are chosen to work in critical arms of government should be people who are morally holy; such civil servants should be models of good moral values and good governance in and outside the executive. The moment we overlook good behaviour, we automatically embrace bad character and, accordingly, negatively affect governance.

In the national government, good governance is only possible when the executive president and his cabinet, bureaucrats and other branches of the executive honour their positions, emulate the holiness of the Lord by their conduct, seeking the guidance of the Lord as they carry out their responsibilities. In the absence of the holiness of the Lord, we will continue complaining about widespread and institutionalised corruption and bad governance in the executive. At this point, let us look into how righteousness facilitates good governance in the executive.

Righteousness

In Proverbs 14:34, the Bible says, "Righteousness exalts a nation, but sin is a disgrace to any people". There are no people under the sun who enjoy sinning. Very often, people do it unknowingly and, as a result, find themselves disgraced. Let us, therefore, keenly study this section of moral purity and see how we can lead our nations in ways of righteousness and reap the benefits that go with it. As referred to earlier, righteousness is one of the moral attributes of God. This indicates that He is just and upright. Similarly, man is said to be righteous when he does what is right, just and good.

No one can achieve true righteousness by his own effort. One must put their faith in Christ to be counted righteous by God and to begin to live a life of righteousness by his (Christ's) power.

The Importance of the Righteousness of a President

A president who fashions his personal character and social relationships after God's righteousness is a living temple of the holy Lord, an advocate of good moral values and good governance. All leaders whose lives are indwelt by God automatically become righteous and successful leaders. God helps them succeed; but He does not associate Himself with corrupt heads of state.

For example, with the help of God, the righteous president embraces and defends all acceptable moral values. Such a head of state speaks and acts morally as he discharges his national duties and pursues the national vision. God's righteousness becomes his guide in leadership. Both God and the entire nation delight in his leadership, but Satan and his evil forces are not happy because they are unable to pursue their agenda under such circumstances. The righteous leader brings joy to God and his nation, for he not only serves the interests of God but also the entire mankind.

Such a president passionately defends the rights of all human beings, irrespective of the colour of their skin, geographical location and geopolitical and economic status. Leaders who are after God's own heart are, of course, as rare as gemstones.

But let's now see the other side of the coin. An unrighteous president is, accordingly, a destroyer of God's image, a destroyer of himself, a destroyer of his family, a destroyer of his nation and a destroyer of mankind. He is an agent of Satan, masquerading as harmless but vile inside and poised to destroy God's people.

Let's pause and ask ourselves pertinent questions here: Do we expect an unrighteous president to mainstream good moral values? Do we expect him to contribute to good governance? Just hold your answers at this point, and let me first share with you my own viewpoints.

First of all, an unrighteous leader has no place for the righteous God in his life because God does not live in an environment of unrighteousness. God is the true source of righteousness. He hates wicked people but loves the righteous. As Solomon says in Prov.15:9: "The Lord detests the way of the wicked, but he loves those who pursue righteousness." And in the absence of both God and His righteousness in the president's life, his mind becomes an empty room, ready for occupation by Satan and all his evil forces, unless God graciously intervenes to extricate him from the snare.

Finding himself under the direct influence of Satan, the unrighteous leader indulges in all manner of acts of the flesh. He treats his family members and government officials insensitively. He also violates the rights of the general public in and outside his national boundaries. As a result, he lives and governs with constant fear because the undesirable effects of his unrighteous leadership make him a likely candidate for the International Criminal Court (ICC) to answer questions in respect of inhumane acts.

What is the scriptural basis for requiring that a national leader conducts himself righteously? Lord expects the president to be involved in righteous acts. To be righteous like God, the president should require that his people do only what is right and what will ultimately have a positive effect upon those whom he governs. Also, his actions should be in accordance with the laws of the land. He is to conduct himself the way he expects of others. Because the president is righteous, obeying his nation's law, his people can trust him and not fear to enter into any pact with him. Joseph, the son of Jacob, is one of the holy rulers of the Bible who lived as God wanted and, as a result, earned people's liking.

Joseph, oozing with self-assurance emanating from a personal knowledge of the Lord, survived and even prospered where most people would have failed. His quiet wisdom and confidence in the Lord led him to win the hearts of everyone he met. Joseph, who rose from slavery to prime minister of Egypt, was known for righteousness. He was spiritually sensitive and through God's guidance prepared a nation to survive a famine that would have wiped out his people, Israel.

As pointed out earlier, the president should discharge his executive tasks guided by God's righteousness. He should come across as the cornerstone of God's righteousness within the executive by teaching the nation to seek the righteousness of God. He must diligently pursue divine righteousness. As the Psalmist says in Ps. 89:14, "Righteousness and justice are the foundation of your throne…" Yes, righteousness and justice, among other pertinent moral values, are the sure cornerstones of righteous leadership. Many nations in the world have good, self-imposed leaders but who are not necessarily righteous. So they are eventually brought down to their knees by the righteous Lord who does not entertain sinners because sin is a disgrace to any people. Righteous leaders are the leaders our world pines for today.

In line with God's will, and as democracy demands, the person who becomes president should be the prerogative of people who exercise their right to choose righteous leaders through the ballot box. In other words, it is the duty of the national citizens to choose a person of high moral behaviour to lead them as president. You have no right to complain about the challenges that follow after you elect an unrighteous person to lead you. After all, how do you expect good governance from him?

A righteous president is the actual torchbearer for good governance in the executive. Leaders must not merely talk about godly righteousness but also practise what they preach. Without God's righteousness in the life of the president, it is of no help for him to speak of good governance in the state.

Besides other vital leadership qualities, our world thirsts for righteous leaders to take us back to God's will for the betterment of mankind and also for God's glory. However, for the president to excel in his duties as the torchbearer for good governance that is guided by God's righteousness, he needs to have his cabinet members work with him as co-torchbearers for good moral values and good governance.

Importance of Righteousness of the Cabinet

A good cabinet is the one in which the behaviour and social relationships of members are guided by righteousness. The presence of righteousness in their lives is the sure evidence of their oneness with the righteous Lord, for no one can attain godly righteousness without the help of God, the actual source of righteousness. And when they have God in their lives, there is no room for Satan and his evil forces. With God in them and they in God, they are able to pursue good moral values and shun all appearance of evil in their daily activities.

A righteous cabinet joins hands with the president and address national issues in a righteous way. They value and safeguard national and individual rights in the community of nations. Under their leadership, people enjoy their national sovereignty, peace, and liberty. Under their leadership, the gap between the poor and the rich in terms of income is considerably narrowed, with all citizens enjoying equal rights before the law. Their strong support of the president is clear evidence of his success. Together with their president, they relentlessly extend an enabling hand to the other two arms of the government to coordinate and harmonize their activities. A cabinet made up of righteous people is the real torchbearer for moral excellence and good governance in and outside the executive.

But a nation in which majority of members of the cabinet are corrupt is a disadvantaged country, which operates and lives without God's guidance. It is the nation where the rights of the people, especially the poor majority, are trampled over by the rich minority. In such a nation, the gap between the poor and the rich keeps increasing, and good moral values are traded for acts of sinful nature. It is a nation that is ruled by Satan and his evil forces because Satan and his demons thrive in an environment of unrighteousness. Such a cabinet is destined to fail itself and its national president, and it is likely to eventually drag the nation into the realm of despair.

What are the general expectations placed upon the cabinet? Just like in the case of the president, the Lord expects members of the cabinet to be key contributors to good governance in and outside the executive. The president's righteousness alone is not enough; members of the cabinet are the ones who do the donkey work within the executive organ, and their daily actions must be in line with the state law. They should conduct themselves in accordance with what they expect of others. If members of the cabinet are righteous, measuring up to the yardstick of God's righteousness, people can sincerely trust them and be not afraid to enter into a relationship with them.

Biblically, we believe that members of the cabinet are, unless they are spiritually insensitive and do not know what they are doing, empowered by the Lord to do His work for the common good of His people and for His own glory, for it is written, "... for the authorities are God's servants, who give their full time to governing" (Rom. 13:6). They do not hold the positions they hold so as to realize their selfish aspirations but for the interest of the nation.

But unless they embrace divine righteousness, they will not rightly fulfil their national obligations. Our world yearns not only for highly qualified leaders but also for Christ-like leaders who drink from an oasis of God's righteousness.

In order for us to have righteous men and women working in our cabinets, it is important for the president and the relevant bodies to be guided by moral values as they make appointments. Preference should be given to people who have submitted their personal conduct and relationship to God's righteousness.

Cabinet members are the right co-torchbearers for good governance in the executive if they are wholeheartedly yielded to God. God requires righteous leaders to lead His people along the path of righteousness. The importance of the cabinet in the life of any nation compels me to wind up this section with the following challenge: Give me a righteous cabinet, and I will thrust the nation very far from the devilish and corrupt cabinet. Righteous cabinet members are a sure blessing from God for any state or people, but an immoral cabinet is a total disgrace for any people or state.

But in order for both the president and his cabinet to shine as enabling torchbearers for good governance within the executive, the bureaucrats and others in the executive should also embrace and practise God's righteousness.

Significance of Righteousness in Bureaucrats

Righteous bureaucrats are a sure blessing to the nation. They base their personal behaviour and social relationships on the concrete rock of God's righteousness. This is a pointer to their union with the Lord as well as their separation from Satan and all his evil forces. Part of their routine administrative functions is fighting vigorously against corruption, and their righteousness does make them successful in whatever they do. For they ensure that their words and deeds are in line with God's righteousness. The rights of the people and the aspirations of the nation always come before their personal interests. They are the solid shoulders that hold and uplift the president and the cabinet. Righteous bureaucrats are valuable and rare to find, for they are the real torchbearers of good moral values and good governance.

But most bureaucrats are unrighteous because they practise corruption and live beyond their means. They put their interests first at the expense of national interests. They have no moral compulsion to seek to do well in their work of fighting against national ills. But why do they behave like that? First of all, unrighteous bureaucrats lack God's righteousness in their individual lives. As such, they have no God in their lives, the actual source of righteousness. This makes them vulnerable to all kinds of satanic influences, and this makes them love the acts of the flesh more than the fruit of the Spirit. Lacking moral values in their personal lives makes them become perpetrators of evil and bad governance. The reason there is so much suffering in our world is because of the many unrighteous bureaucrats in the nations.

Bureaucrats are the mandated implementers of government decisions. Therefore, their conduct, as they carry out their obligations, demands particular attention. This is because if they are morally bad, they can do much harm to the nation. The opposite would happen if they conducted themselves righteously. They are supposed to lead God's people by helping them realize their aspirations as a nation rather than pursuing their own self-centred interests.

All governments are instituted of the Lord, and He wants people to be submissive to the authorities because they exist to do His will. Apostle Paul commands, "Everyone must submit himself to the governing authorities, for there is no authority except that which God has established. The authorities that exist have been established by God" (Rom. 13: 1).

This is to say that everyone in the government office is put there by the Lord to serve Him by serving His people. But of course, we know that not all those holding national offices are doing God's will; some government officers are serving themselves instead of serving God. But God knows how to deal with such selfish people because the wise man says, "He who oppresses the poor shows contempt for their Maker, but whoever is kind to the needy honors God" (Prov. 14:31).

Because of the bureaucrats' importance in the executive, and since they are appointed by God to lead His people, the Lord expects all of them to emulate His righteousness. The bureaucrats are said to be righteous if their actions accord with the state law. They should treat the others the way they expect others to treat them. Only when the bureaucrats in the executive organ conduct themselves righteously can we correctly term them as co-torchbearers for good governance. The nation is not only looking for technocrats but also righteous bureaucrats to serve the Lord by serving His people. Of course, that means that if we want to have righteous senior civil servants, those in charge of hiring and recruiting must diligently look for men and women who are morally upright.

Even the other branches of the executive, such as the armed forces, should have their conduct guided by God's righteousness as they give their services in their respective positions. Moreover, the Lord expects them to require of their juniors to do only what is right and what will have a positive effect upon those under their rule.

If all the branches of the executive embrace God's righteousness as their foundational moral code, discharging their obligations as guided by God, they will automatically merit their title as co-torchbearers for good governance within and beyond the executive. All those who work within the executive arm of the government should put on God's righteousness.

Needless to say, in order to have righteous bureaucrats and righteous members of the armed forces, those in charge of the recruitment of such civil servants should go for men and women of moral integrity, civil servants whose personal character is in sync with God's righteousness.

Justice

"**B**lessed are they who maintain justice, who constantly do what is right" (Ps.106:3). Aware that maintaining justice in our daily lives brings blessings, who wouldn't want to seek it? We hanker for justice in our individual lives, in our families, in our churches and, more importantly, in our governments. Justice is the same as fairness or righteousness. Justice or fairness is the act of rendering and enforcing a fair verdict, whether of damnation or reward. It is one of the attributes of God, who gives abundant mercy without going outside of the real application of justice. God's trademark is justice, and His will is that all government agents adhere to His standards.

The Importance of Justice in the Life of a President

Many national leaders in our corrupt and immoral world preach but do not practise justice, the reason being that justice is not a part of their personal lives. But when a head of state's behaviour and social relationships conform to God's justice, God showers him, his family and the entire nation with blessings. He becomes the living temple of God's Spirit but a disgrace to Satan. His friendship with the just Lord helps him discern and internalise good moral values. Such a president's leadership ensures that all members of the public have access to and enjoy justice regardless of their religious affiliation, socio-economic or political position. The leader becomes the national and international advocate and protector of justice and other aspects of good moral values, the upshot being good governance. Over time, those under him and the general public embrace justice as well. Such is the leader after God's own heart.

However, when the president does not establish his personality and relationships on justice, he lives and leads without God's help, for a just Lord does not like to associate

Himself with the unjust. Eventually, this kind of leader finds himself under satanic control. Henceforth, the unjust president leads and interacts with the public unjustly. For instance, he may deny justice to the national citizens, especially the common people. Even after national laws are enacted and promulgated, they do not have the same effects on the people. Such a leader is not in good terms with his followers, especially those who love justice.

This is the kind of president who is always above the law as long as he is in power. Unless God intervenes in his life, such a leader becomes a curse to his nation and to mankind as a whole.

But what are God's expectations from a state president so far as divine justice is concerned? Let me begin with the following biblical quotation: "By justice a king gives a country stability, but one who is greedy for bribes tears it down" (Prov. 29:4). Mr. President, what legacy do you want to leave behind? Do you love to execute justice and bring stability to your nation, or do you love to pervert justice and thus, tear down your nation in the process? Whatever the case, the Creator of all creatures, including yourself of course, has the final word, for He says, "For I, the Lord, love justice; I hate robbery and iniquity" (Isa. 61:8a).

In order to exercise justice within and outside the executive branch of the government, the Lord requires the president to take divine justice as the guide for his moral character. As part of exercising justice, the Lord requires him to be careful to reward both evil and good because he must be fair in the application of the national law. He should avoid favouritism and, instead, let it be known that justice should be done to everybody, irrespective of one's station in life.

Lack of justice in the government circles results in inequality when it comes to developing different parts of the nation. Some states become more developed than others. For instance, in the nation of the Sudan, it is common to hear people talking about developed and marginalised areas. And this disparity in development has been the cause of the many civil wars that the nation has seen since 1958 or thereabouts.

The absence of godly justice in most of the national governments has also led to unfair distribution of the national cake, making the favoured people richer and the masses poorer. The same lack of the divine justice in the executive is behind the stately mansions owned by a few rich amid sprawling informal settlements in major cities where the masses live in squalor. Injustice is also the cause of the increasing number of 'street children' in many big cities. Some of these 'street children' have matured and become fathers and mothers while still suffering the indignity of homelessness, and this led to the existence of street families. But what are governments saying about this widespread injustice?

The president ought to ensure that divine justice is accessible to all the people in the country. He himself should practise justice as he leads the nation on behalf of God. In the book of Amos, the divine command is: "But let justice role on like a river, righteousness like a never-failing stream!" (Amos 5:24) The president who upholds God's justice in his individual life and as he governs is the worthy torchbearer for good governance in and outside the executive.

The government under such a just president will be able to create an atmosphere of prosperity, justice, equality and love among the people. His leadership will also contribute to narrowing the gap between the rich and the poor. He will also fight vigorously for equal allocation of resources for national development without considering ethnic background, creed, socio-economic or political status. That way, he will attract God's blessings upon the nation. Actually, our world is crying for leaders who yield themselves to divine justice to guide their thoughts, words and even deeds.

But unless we become careful to elect the right leaders—those who base their personal behaviour and social relationships on God's justice—we will forever be dogged by poor governance. Let's therefore, invest time and thought to appraise those who are seeking political office before we give them our votes and thus, mandate them to lead us.

But a just president is alone not enough to bring about good governance in the executive without the help of a just cabinet.

The Importance of Justice in the Cabinet

A cabinet whose members are not guided by divine justice is sure to fail the president and the entire nation, since it operates without the backing of God. Such a cabinet is used by Satan and his evil forces to carry out his wicked plans. Such a cabinet does not serve the interests of the general public, and it also denies people, especially the weak and the poor, access to justice. Among other evils, its members do contribute to unequal allocation of development resources and in oppressing and marginalising the poor. They put their individual interests above national interests as evidenced by the fact that they will not hesitate to be involved in corruption. But what else do you expect from an unjust cabinet, anyway?

Cabinet members ought to emulate God when it comes to matters of justice, whether involving the nation or individuals. The just Lord says, "I will make justice the measuring line and righteousness the plumb line" (Isa. 28:17a). As a loyal cabinet member, what guides the way you conduct your life and execute your national duties? Our God uses justice and righteousness as the yardstick in his dealings with you and others. And in order for His divine justice to be experienced by His people, He expects members of the cabinet to fully embrace it and implement their national activities on the basis of justice. Justice is to be the yardstick by which they reward both evil and good, for God asserts:

> Know therefore that the Lord your God is God; he is the faithful God, keeping his covenant of love to a thousand generations of those who love him and keep his commands. But those who hate him he will repay to their face by destruction; he will not be slow to repay to their face those who hate him (Deut. 7:9).

The cabinet should guarantee justice to all the citizens in spite of their political affiliation, socio-economic status or religious affiliation. They should treat all citizens equally and allocate the nation's resources equitably to all regions. They should inject the essence of the divine justice into the national blood stream by modelling justice in themselves. They are also to stand shoulder-to-shoulder with the executive president in the fair application of the godly justice within and outside national borders. By so doing, they fulfil their national and spiritual obligations because they are actually appointed by the Lord to lead His people in line with His will.

Of course, in order for us to realise good governance and good moral values in the cabinet, the national president and other relevant authorities must appoint people of high moral values, people especially keen on applying justice, to serve in the cabinet. Such people will promote morality and thus, dispense with poor governance in and outside the national executive organ. We should not deliberately staff our executive organ with unjust men and women and expect justice to exist therein!

The cabinet becomes a co-torchbearer for good governance in the executive if the conduct of its individual members is guided by divine justice and carries out all its national tasks in the light of God's justice. That is the sort of cabinet that we need.

Let God's justice be the cornerstone of the executive branch of the government for the national peace to prevail, for God's blessings to shower down on the land, for national prosperity to thrive, for brotherhood to abound among the citizens, for cordial relationship to exist within national boundaries and for good governance to thrive in the nation. The cabinet members should wear the crown of the divine justice and work as the co-torchbearers for good governance in and outside the executive.

But divine justice will not result in good governance in the executive and in the rest of the government unless the bureaucrats too are pursuing God's justice as they perform their state duties.

Importance of Justice in the Lives of Bureaucrats

Given the important role of the bureaucracy, if bureaucrats lack God's justice in their individual lives, the whole nation is doomed, for the absence of justice in their dealings means the absence of God in them. Any nation whose civil servants lack godly justice in their lives is known for widespread violation of human rights and all sorts of ills. In such a nation, the weak and the poor are systematically oppressed and subjected to dehumanising treatment by the very few strong and rich people. By failing God and the masses, the unjust bureaucrats bring failure to themselves, to their cabinet and to the president as well. And the reason is because they are enslaved and blinded by the evil forces. Of course, it would be asking too much to expect unjust bureaucrats to deliver good governance in their country.

"Evil men do not understand justice, but those who seek the Lord understand it fully" (Pr. 28:5). Do you, as a good and seasoned bureaucrat, know the importance of justice in your life? If so, do you live out or practise what you are aware of daily? As you reflect on your life to know the answer, you should remember that for good governance to exist, justice is necessary, not just from the president and the cabinet but also from the bureaucrats. The executive president, the cabinet and the bureaucrats should join their hands, hearts and minds together and work diligently towards the realization of good governance within and outside the executive.

The impartiality of the bureaucrats should manifest in their righteousness before they demand the same from the other people. They must practise what they preach; they must show that they are righteous before they require the others to fashion their character after God's character. The bureaucrats are to show fairness in the administration of justice by refraining from portraying any favouritism. People are to receive what they deserve, whether bad or good.

In terms of the government hierarchy, bureaucrats are nearer to the common people. Therefore, they should be more conscious of the need to be just as they deal with the general population daily. They have more opportunities of practising justice, as they come in direct contact with people in the course of implementing government policies. In the course of their work, they should be impartial, irrespective of people's socio-economic, political, racial or religious background. Really, bureaucrats are very significant in the eyes of God. He put them there to serve Him by serving His people justly as civil servants. But if they are unjust in their words, deeds and thoughts and only work to satisfy their own selfish interests in the name of carrying out their national duties, the entire nation is doomed. What do you think?

The bureaucrats become true co-torchbearers for good governance if they wholeheartedly discharge their duties under the guidance of God's justice. In our governments, we are in great need of just men and women to be bureaucrats, people who have completely surrendered skills and abilities to

God for divine ability to practise justice. These are the kind of men and women who live out the Scripture in Amos 5:24 that urges people to let justice flow down like a mighty stream and righteousness like a never-failing river.

Also, God expects to see divine justice practised in other arms, the armed forces, of the executive. They, too, are expected to embrace divine justice as the cornerstone of their moral values and through which they are to execute their national duties. None of the personnel in the executive is, of course, exempted from practising justice in the course of their work. It is not possible to speak of good governance in the executive or in the entire government without all government officials practising godly justice in the course of their work.

Any appointments or recruitments of bureaucrats and other senior personnel in the armed forces ought to be guided by God's justice to ensure that persons of high moral values are placed in the key places. If those who base their conduct on God's justice are chosen, good moral values will find room in the civil service and lead to good governance.

In conclusion, good governance is only possible in and outside the executive when the executive president, the cabinet, the bureaucrats and other agents of the executive embrace justice as the guide to their personal conduct and in discharging their duties. They are to work as the torchbearers for good governance in the executive in the light of God's justice.

Not only that, for good governance to pervade the executive in the light of moral purity, all those who work there must uphold, cherish and practise holiness, righteousness and justice in their personal lives. They are also to base their social relationships and the way they carry out their national duties on the same ingredients of moral purity. People who are known for moral purity are the ones who have what it takes to bring good governance and acceptable moral values into national executive organ worldwide.

But for people to realise good governance within and outside the executive organ, let us see in the next chapter how the three dimensions of integrity can to enhance good governance when embraced by all agents working in the executive.

Chapter 2
Integrity in the Executive

For people to realize good governance in and outside the executive, all members of the executive must base their personal character and official duties on the three aspects of integrity.

God's Word in Prov. 11:3 says: "The integrity of the upright guides them, but the unfaithful are destroyed by their duplicity." All over the world, the nations that are led by people of integrity enjoy socio-economic and political prosperity as well as enduring peace. But we are also familiar with millions of people who are suffering greatly as a result of being deceived by their national leaders. In this chapter of the book, I seek to prove that it is possible to maintain integrity and enjoy life and intimate communion with our God, and it is also possible to follow dishonesty and be beneficiaries of the attendant curse from the just Lord, with regrettable consequences upon our lives and the lives of our children's children. The choice is yours.

Simply put, integrity refers to a high standard of moral excellence, honesty, wholeness or soundness. In the words of Richard Kriegbaum, "Integrity is being what I claim to be and doing what I promise to do. A great leader must demonstrate personal integrity."[4] In the following section, I will explore the realization of good governance in different areas of the executive organs of the government by embracing the following three aspects of integrity: genuineness, veracity, and faithfulness.

Genuineness

Genuineness refers to the very state of reality or authenticity of anything. Things are just the way they are, just the way God explicitly and simply says about Himself, "…I AM WHO I AM…" (Exod.3:14). He is God, period. This is because saying more than that will contradict His real nature. What about you? Do you present yourself before God and people just the way you are? As a matter of fact, some people don't know who they are, and so they fail to genuinely present themselves before God and others. But if they understood themselves well enough, they would discover the bad side of themselves and attempt to hide that part of what they hate concerning themselves. Also, people don't like others to understand what they do and what they don't. This inherited un-genuineness of man is a part of the reason why people who are seeking to start families or business often fail to get the right partners or the right employee for a certain job.

But the omniscient Lord understands all of us and loves us just the way we are, so far as our physical looks are concerned. God loves people to the extent of welcoming them to come before His throne of grace to bring their burdens and sins that they would want forgiven so that they can start enjoying the royal fellowship with Him. For you and I to attain self-esteem and genuine self-acceptance so that we can enjoy life, let's shun evil and embrace honesty.

---

4   Kriegbaum, Richard. Leadership Prayers. Wheaton, Illinois: Tyndale House Publishers, INC., 1998.

Let us now look into how the genuineness of the president can promote good governance within and outside the executive branch of the government.

Importance of the Genuineness of a President

"The Lord detests lying lips, but he delights in men who are truthful" (Prov. 12:22). Mr. President, are you one of the very few truthful men and women, or you are one of the many liars? Kindly give yourself a genuine answer to this all-important question.

The president is the national leader who is installed on the state throne by the power of the Almighty God to lead his people in line with God's will. He is there to safeguard and fulfil the aspirations of people as a nation by serving God through serving his own people. A Christ-like leader is but a servant of the people and does not use his power to put his own narrow and selfish interests above national interests; his governance is a sacrificial effort to help his people realize their national aspirations.

However, our world leaders often let down God and His people by failing to fulfil the primary reasons for which they have been given the leadership rod. It is unfortunate that many do not know that their election was sanctioned by God, since Apostle Paul writing to Christians in Rome says that "… for there is no authority except that which God has established. The authorities that exist have been established by God" (Rom. 13:1b).

But many national leaders nowadays do not acknowledge God's role in their appointment. Instead, they believe that they are there in political power due to their own luck, expertise, wealth, physical strength and power connections, among other factors. Such 'self-made' leaders do not care about the interests of the nation at large. Instead, they pursue their own selfish aspirations at the expense of other people. Also, they seek self-glorification rather than seeking to glorify God.

As long as their own interests are taken care of, these 'self-made' leaders entertain the mistaken perception that good governance has taken place within and outside the national boundaries. Such are the presidents who refuse to relinquish power because they are fully aware of their misdeeds and are afraid of the dreadful consequences should they be subjected to the legal process. They live like person who is sitting on a bomb that could be detonated any time but which will not go off as long as he sits on it. That is why such a leader is left with no option but to continue in power for fear of what would befall him should he become a civilian. But what do you do as a leader to pre-empt such a situation? Answer: Lead with integrity so that when your time of exiting comes, you will have nothing to fear; if anything, you will welcome the life of a civilian joyfully and enjoy the respect that citizens accord a loved former head of state.

Today, the world is full of leaders who seem not to know who they really are and what their role is. If they don't really understand who they are, who, apart from the omniscient Lord, can show them who they are? A president is the rallying point of the nation; so he is supposed to completely understand himself and his role before he can help his family members and the rest of his countrymen.

When the president hides a part of who he is, he misleads himself, his party members and the rest of the nation. Worse still, he makes a fool of God. For example, his life is full of a lot of pretences and the attendant regrets. He is one person in his private life but quite another in public. Let me make myself clearer here. I am not saying that he should take his domestic mess to the public. What I am saying is that his personality should be characterized by consistency. He should be a man who emulates God, one who qualifies to say, "I am who I am". Lacking original development ideas, such a leader rehashes past development proposals to try to redeem his poor image. He is ever after compliments to prop his fragile ego. Unfortunately, such people are vulnerable victims of flatterers, especially ladies with ill motive.

What are the people's general expectations of the president so far as genuineness is concerned? To further stress the importance of integrity, Henry T. and Richard Blackaby have said, "Integrity means being consistent in one's behaviour under every circumstance, including unguarded moments."[5] The primary aspect of the divine integrity is God's genuineness, which shows that the Lord is a real God. His genuineness and His reality go together; He is exactly what He appears to be. Accordingly, the Lord expects His moral agents to maintain their own true genuineness under all conditions. The national leader must bear his genuineness, both in private and in public as he leads his people in line with God's will and public expectations. He should not imitate behaviour that is not a part of him. The genuineness of God should be the mark of his own moral character and the foundation of his leadership as he leads his people in line with God's will for the benefit of the entire nation.

The president can only become a true torchbearer for good governance in and outside the executive branch of the government if he adopts the genuineness of God as the firm basis of the moral code of his conduct and the only yardstick with which he measures his leadership within and outside the country.

But how is it possible to get such a genuine leader? It is the duty

---

5   T., Henry, and Richard Blackaby. Spiritual Leadership: The Interactive Study. Nashville, Tennessee: Broadman and Holman Publishers, 2006.

of the citizens of the nation to diligently vet and elect a person of high moral integrity, one who wears God's genuineness as his moral necklace, and put him in charge of their nation. And God is more than willing to help them as they do so. Our world is not looking for chameleon-like leaders; what it seriously requires are Christ-like leaders whose genuineness endures throughout their life time. Choose and follow a genuine leader, and you will reap the fruit that comes with his kind of character!

Nevertheless, the genuineness of the president alone cannot ensure good governance in the executive; he needs the input of cabinet members who have also embraced genuineness.

Significance of the Genuineness of the Cabinet

The genuineness of cabinet members is also necessary if good governance is to be realized. Their strength or weakness determines the strength or the weakness of the executive organ. As a result, it is imperative that we pay full attention to the true nature or authenticity of the cabinet members who are the president's co-torchbearers for good governance.

Nowadays, it is hard to establish the authenticity of many cabinet members in governments in different parts of the world because they behave like chameleon when they are implementing executive orders and in the way they relate with people on a day-to-day basis. For example, when they are not in political position, some members of the cabinet behave differently than when they are in politics. When they are holding executive posts, they behave in a different way from the way they behaved before. Before assuming office, they come across as peaceful, honest and friendly, but as soon as they get into politics, they distant themselves from other people, show their true colours and begin to behave dishonestly towards themselves and towards fellow countrymen.

When majority members of the cabinet lack the essence of

God's genuineness in their lives, they conceal their true self and instead embrace the unhealthy spirit of pretence. Needless to say, this unhealthy spirit of pretence is really Satan's deception spirit. This spirit makes the cabinet members not operate in transparent and accountable manner. Their words, deeds and even thoughts are, instead, acceptable in the kingdom of darkness. Since such people are not genuine to themselves, the cabinet members are not genuine to God, to their president and to the general public as well. Over time, the cabinet members become agents of the evil forces, with no sense of good moral values and good governance at all in their lives.

Blackaby says, "Employees have counted honesty in their leaders as more important than vision, competence, accomplishments, and the ability to inspire others."[6] In corroborating this quotation, it is imperative to say that our leaders are required by God to be very honest when dealing with themselves, when dealing with their Creator and when dealing with others. As we very well know, God's genuineness is the basic element of His integrity. Hence, He requires this to be a vital character of the cabinet members. Their character should reflect their genuineness before both man and God. They should not imitate false behaviour as they discharge their national responsibilities or in the way they relate with their fellow countrymen.

It is an inescapable responsibility of the president and others who work with him to choose men and women whose personal character and relationships are guided by God's genuineness to serve in the cabinet. The cabinet members can only become true co-torchbearers for good governance in the executive when they uphold the divine genuineness as the ethical basis of their personal character and discharge their national duties in the light of God's own genuineness. Our world needs cabinet

---

6 Ibid.,Blackaby, 84.

members whose genuineness reflects their true identity. If we choose men and women of disguised personalities to occupy cabinet positions, we set ourselves up for doom!

But apart from the genuineness of both the chief executive and the cabinet members, it is necessary for the bureaucrats to also embrace this important virtue if good governance is to be realized.

Importance of the Genuineness of Bureaucrats

For important government projects to succeed, they are put under the supervision of efficient, effective bureaucrats. But such bureaucrats are hard to come by, and, very often, governments are forced to do with ineffective, inefficient and incoherent bureaucrats, with disastrous results of course.

Many bureaucrats do not measure up to the definition of the word "bureaucrat", for they are clearly too ill-equipped to hold any government office. When put in power, such people are steeped in their selfish interests but pretending to serve public interest. After all, some of them may be in such a position, not through merit but through leveraging connections or through nepotism. Any government that allows such incompetent bureaucrats to operate shows lack of direction and the stagnating of political and socio-economic progress.

When the bureaucrats lack the essence of God's genuineness in their personal lives, that means God is not in control of them. And the absence of God in their lives makes their minds vulnerable to the invasion and occupation of Satan and his evil forces. As a result, these bureaucrats behave unrealistically towards the general public and the national leader by what they say or do. They shun all good moral values and, instead, rationalise and embrace acts of sinful nature. As unworthy civil servants, they draw their people away from the path of national goal through different forms of deception. Just as they are capable of failing themselves, they are capable of bringing about a "a failed state".

In order to avert this dangerous situation, God would want genuine bureaucrats to be delegated the task of carrying out important responsibilities. While doing their work within and outside the executive wing of the government, bureaucrats should be real in what they do, in what they say and in how they think. Their skilfulness and genuineness should be clearly seen by all before they are given the executive roles.

Bureaucrats can emerge as real co-torchbearers for good governance in the executive if they genuinely base their own moral character on God's genuineness and reflect this actual and divine genuineness in their individual lives as well as in doing their national duties. Instead of blowing their own trumpet, let others see and praise the genuineness of the bureaucrats. Ineffective bureaucrats in the executive do not serve any purpose in the national government. What we require are genuine bureaucrats who maintain their true image under all circumstances.

The existence of real good governance in the executive requires that governments agents like armed forces embrace divine genuineness, too. It is by this that they are to benchmark their moral values on divine genuineness as they execute their national obligations. Our key national leaders should therefore, exercise care and honesty in their recruitment of people to hold key positions so as to put men and women of high integrity, especially God's genuineness, in the government. God wants all the executive officials to be genuine before Him and live genuinely.

It is important that the executive president, the cabinet members, the bureaucrats and workers in other branches of the executive wear the attire of God's genuineness and act as true torchbearers for good governance within and outside the executive part of the government. As a matter of fact, our world badly needs genuine men and women to honestly manage the executive departments of our national governments.

But it is also very vital, if we want to see the real good governance in the executive, to see the same members of the executive embracing veracity as an important part of their lives and critical instrument with which they are to carry out their national duties.

Veracity

Veracity uplifts a nation. It pleases God but displeases dishonest Satan and his evil host. On the other hand, dishonesty undermines a nation. It pleases Satan and his evil forces but displeases the honest Lord.

Since it is one of the significant pillars of the government, God expects the executive organ to be guided by divine veracity in executing its functions. It is to do that through its separate organs such as the president, the cabinet, the bureaucrats, etc.

Under this section, I intend to explore the possible situations in which good governance thrives in the executive branch of the government in the light of God's veracity. Due to the synonymous of veracity with honesty, uprightness, truthfulness and truth, I will use these terms interchangeably in the course of the discussion. Let's see now how the president becomes the torchbearer for good governance in and outside the executive organ when he bases his moral character and social interactions on the sure ground of God's veracity.

Significance of the Veracity of a President

In Proverbs 10:9 the Bible says, "The man of integrity walks securely, but he who takes crooked paths will be found out." For our national leaders to be secure, the prerequisite is sound leadership and ethical conduct. It is common knowledge that the president of a state is a very important person, one who rallies the entire nation towards its vision, mission and strategic objectives for the common good of the entire populace. He is the rallying point in the executive, guiding in the setting of national priorities, crafting policies concerning the allocation of resources and honour as well as in public debate to determine specific approaches to domestic and international affairs. As a result, he should be the kind of person who sees far.

Unfortunately, very often some of the state leaders in the executive are not true to themselves, to God and to their own followers. As a result, it becomes hard for others to believe and follow them. For instance, a leader who lacks the spirit of divine veracity in his personal life is a leader who is totally devoid of moral integrity, since there is no integrity minus honesty. In the absence of integrity in the state leader's life, he cannot have God in his life. Instead, he becomes a slave of the evil forces.

A dishonest president becomes dishonest with himself first before he becomes dishonest with God and other people. His dishonesty starts right from his bedroom and moves with him right to his office. He is dishonest in words, deeds and thoughts. His followers and the general public find it hard to have faith in him and follow his example despite being their national leader. He lets down his family members and the entire nation on many occasions. When the president is a man devoid of integrity, he is without good moral values, leave alone the ability to provide good governance to his people or mankind in general. Are we familiar with such presidents in our world today? How can their moral depravity be addressed?

If their ethical problems arise from lack of God's veracity in their lives, then let them take and wear it (God's veracity) as their noble leadership and personal attire. The president's veracity is very necessary in his setting of national priorities and in his proposing of policies on the allocation of the national resources and honour. Without divine veracity even people of the same nation will not receive an equal share of their national resources or honour from their state leader. His veracity is also needed in guiding him in his daily activities. For any leader to lead successfully, his veracity in dealing with himself and in dealing with others must not be compromised.

It is the sole duty of the citizens of any nation under the sun to choose capable and morally upright leaders, especially the president, to guide them along the path of God's honesty in the pursuit of their national vision. When a nation puts a dishonest person in power, it sets itself on the road to moral doom.

God wants a leader who wears honesty as a sign of his moral excellence. He wants leaders to be honest in all situations, to be truthful, both in what they say and in what they mean by what they say. The leader should present things just the way they are, whether he is speaking of himself or concerning a section of his government. This kind of leadership is what our world is yearning for at the moment.

Most of our governments are under witty and rhetoric leaders, but not truthful ones. "Followers don't expect their leaders to be perfect, but they do expect them to be honest. Both secular and Christian societies realize that integrity is paramount in a leader's life."[7] We seriously need leaders who honestly immerse their leadership expertise deeply in the oasis of divine veracity.

With a national leader who permanently wears the crown of the divine veracity and discharges his national tasks in the light of God's veracity, good governance is assured. Such a leader is the real torchbearer for good governance within and outside the executive. Frankly speaking, give me an honest leader, and I will give you a blessed nation.

---

7 Ibid., Blacaby, 84.

But the president's veracity alone is not sufficient enough to facilitate good governance in the executive; the honesty of the entire cabinet is necessary, too.

Significance of the Veracity of the Cabinet

No matter how honest the executive president may be, his veracity alone is not enough to provide good governance within and outside the boundaries of the executive. This is simply because members of his cabinet are the ones implementing his decisions. Thus, in the absence of their individual veracity, the honesty of the president can just be like a small stone hurled into the middle of an ocean. Of course, I am not saying that his veracity is insignificant in the welfare of the nation. The point I am making here is that if he is backed by an equally honest cabinet, the resulting synergy would be immense, and it would contribute greatly to the realization of good governance.

An honest president can be brought down from power by a dishonest cabinet. For example, if most of the cabinet members lack God's veracity in their personal lives, they act and talk immorally in the course of their work. Even in their dealings with the president, the bureaucrats and other fellow citizens, they are dishonest, both in their dealings and relationship with one another. The president may want to steer the nation towards the right direction, but dishonest cabinet members will make sure that his orders and advice are not followed. And so, instead of following the acceptable and honest route, vested interests make them influence things and end up taking the nation in the opposite direction. They poison the minds and the hearts of the bureaucrats to avoid the path of good moral values and good governance for the sake of the acts of the flesh.

When the cabinet is full of dishonest members, definitely God will not be happy with them and with the entire nation as well. Thus, the president will fail in his leadership in spite of his veracity, and the general masses will suffer the consequences of the evil cabinet. Under the poor leadership of a dishonest cabinet, massive corruption will exist in the economy and politics, with vast national resources finding their way across the national boundaries to private accounts in foreign banks. The concomitant lack of good governance will result in huge foreign debts, a high level of poverty, inadequate medical facilities, low quality of education and, eventually, civil strife.

To pre-empt such an undesirable situation, governments should be manned by honest people, who are known for being truthful as they interact with the members of the public, faithful to God and in their dealings with other members of the cabinet. We want cabinet members who portray things as they actually are, whether they are speaking of themselves or anything to do with their work or the entire nation. The Lord wants them to be honest under all circumstances by being truthful both in what they assert and in what they imply.

But to get these good cabinet members, it is the primary role of the president and other concerned parties to be extremely honest with themselves so as to appoint men and women of good moral character, especially God's veracity, to occupy and manage this vital government branch. Honest cabinet members facilitate good governance in and beyond the executive.

Good governance is only possible within and outside the executive if all men and women working in the cabinet adopt God's veracity as the fundamental cornerstone of their own personal lives and operate as honest co-torchbearers for good governance. Also, good governance is only achievable in and outside the executive when all national activities within the purview of the members of the cabinet are done in the light of God's veracity.

Nevertheless, for true good governance to exist in and

beyond the confines of the executive, bureaucrats need also to wear the gown of God's veracity.

Importance of the Veracity of Bureaucrats

If bureaucrats do not base their individual behaviour and social relationships on the concrete foundation of God's veracity, they will live, talk and act without God in their daily lives. Dishonest bureaucrats deceive themselves, the members of the cabinet, the president and members of the general public. And not just that, they are dishonest towards their Creator, too. The absence of veracity in the lives of most members of the national bureaucracy is a sign of the nation's imminent failure. Many nations, including the newly born nation of the Republic of South Sudan, are struggling to extricate themselves from the tricky snare into which they were thrust by moral dishonesty.

It is important for us to understand that no matter how well both the president and his cabinet members perform in the area of the divine veracity, their truthfulness alone cannot bring about good governance in and outside the executive if there is no slight mention of the divine veracity among the bureaucrats. Definitely, bureaucrats always outnumber the team comprising the chief executive and his whole cabinet. To do away with corruption and mismanagement, therefore, requires that the bureaucrats embrace God's veracity as the standard guide in their work. That way, they will be heeding John the Baptist's warnings, "Tax collectors also came to be baptised. 'Teacher,' "they asked," 'what should we do?' 'Don't collect any more than you are required to', he told them" (Lk. 3:12). The truth is that the more they ask for what is more than necessary, the more they lose their credibility and fling the nation into an abyss of desperation.

God seriously requires the bureaucrats to adopt his divine veracity, first and foremost, as the principal of their own moral code of conduct. This is because unless they personally and completely internalise the essence of the divine veracity into their own lives, they can neither give it out to others nor exercise their national tasks in the light of God's veracity. Whether they talk about themselves or about their work, the bureaucrats, as honest government officials, must present things truthfully. They must be honest in all situations by being truthful both in what they declare and in what they infer.

What our world is after is not clever bureaucrats who only mind personal gain, irrespective of whether the executives are dragging their governments into the sea of corruption. Instead, what the world yearns for is honest and truthful men and women who are known for their divine veracity. It greatly needs bureaucrats who wear the crown of honesty as they carry out their national obligations before God and man.

Bureaucrats can become co-torchbearers for good governance in and outside the executive if their lives are guided by the divine veracity and when they realize that they are God's loyal servants who are put there to serve Him by serving His people honestly. We can speak of there being good governance in the executive if justice is clearly evident among all the citizens regardless of the colour of their skin, religious and political affiliation and where they come from geographically. Good governance is obvious in and outside the executive if all people are treated by the bureaucrats as God's children and all the national duties carried out as if they are being done unto the Lord. Our desire is for people who are known for their veracity to work as God's stewards in the executive for the common good of the human race and for the glory of the Lord as well.

In the same way, other parts of the executive - such as armed forces - are expected to uphold God's veracity to guide their personal lives and in carrying out their national tasks. The following Scripture shows the kind of moral behaviour John the

Baptist demanded from the armed forces: "Then some soldiers asked him, 'And what should we do?' He replied, 'don't extort money and don't accuse people falsely – be content with your pay'" (Lk. 3:14). The Lord wants them to maintain their veracity as they relate to each other, as they commune with their God and as they interact with the members of the public. They are not the enemies of the people but their protectors.

These other branches of the executive can become good co-torchbearers for good governance in the executive if they wholeheartedly embrace God's veracity as the basic guide to their individual lives to govern their personal character while discharging their national duties for the benefit of the whole nation.

In order for us to see good governance being practised by the bureaucracy and other agencies, those who are responsible for the national appointment and recruitment exercises must be people of high moral values. This moral quality will help them execute this vital role in the light of God's veracity so as to put ethically good people in important positions for the common good of the entire nation. Getting immoral people into the government is the direct result of recruitment exercises and appointments made by immoral and corrupt people.

In summary, for good governance to prevail in the executive branch of the government, for all the people to enjoy equal access to their national resources and equal protection, and for the nation to receive God's blessings, the executive president, the cabinet, the bureaucrats and other branches of the executive must put God in their personal lives to guide all what they do. They should take the divine veracity as the standard of their moral character and to guide them in carrying out their national duties. Their veracity will qualify them to be the real co-torchbearers for good governance in and outside the executive.

Let us now see the role of divine faithfulness, the last element of God's integrity, in the executive in good governance.

Faithfulness

Faithfulness means unwavering loyalty to somebody or to a cause. It is about being firm in obedience, absolutely loyal and practising faith. God is faithful to Himself in regard to His personality as well as to all His actions, His words and deeds. His promises stand forever and ever because unfaithfulness is not part of His nature. Erickson said, "If God's genuineness is a matter of his being true and veracity is his telling of the truth, then his faithfulness means that he proves true."[8]

Because of His faithfulness, God expects His people to base their moral character on the clear foundation of the divine faithfulness in dealing among themselves and as they relate with their faithful Creator. He expects believers to emulate His faithfulness. They should not throw their words thoughtlessly, and when they give their words, they are to remain faithful to them as it is written, "When you make a vow to God, do not delay in fulfilling it. He has no pleasure in fools; fulfil your vow. It is better not to vow than to make a vow and not fulfil it" (Eccl .5:4-5).

In this part of the book, I wish to examine some vital preconditions which should be satisfied to permit good governance to flourish in the executive branch of the government. Good governance and acceptable moral values can exist within and outside the executive when the president, the cabinet, the bureaucracy and associate agents base their ethical character and social relationships on the solid rock of God's faithfulness.

---

8 Erickson, Milliard J. Christian Theology, Unabridged, One-Volume Edition. Grand Rapids, Michigan: Baker Book House, 1996.

Significance of the Faithfulness of a President

Who has ever experienced true happiness by associating himself with or following an unfaithful leader? If you answer in the affirmative, it shows that you too are unfaithful. After all, a common proverb says that birds of a feather flock together.

First of all, a faithless president is devoid of faith in God, faith in himself, faith in his wife and children or faith in any other human being. Accordingly, those who follow him contend with enormous setbacks and the attendant regrets. This is because the one they are following cannot keep his words and account for his actions. He says one thing and does the other. Also, he changes with change in circumstances. Lacking the essence of faithfulness in his life means he lacks the spirit of moral integrity as well.

Yet faithless people can camouflage themselves as long as they commoners, but a faithless president is easy to find out and also dangerous for people to follow. It is impossible for a faithless president to instil the essence of divine faithfulness into the bloodstream of government systems.

For the state leader to shine as the true torchbearer for good governance, he must adopt God's faithfulness as the cornerstone of his personal character. A good leader needs to prove himself truthful in words, deeds and thoughts as he leads God's people. He must keep all his promises, not committing himself to do something which he may eventually be unable to do. This is because the Lord requires those who believe in Him to emulate His faithfulness. The executive president is not to throw his words thoughtlessly as he seeks to emphasize points. But once words come out of his mouth, he is under obligation to honour them. God's Word says, "When you make a vow to God, do not delay in fulfilling it. He has no pleasure in fools; fulfil your vow. It is better not to vow than to make a vow and not fulfil it" (Eccl. 5:4-5). Once a leader makes a vow, either to God or to any of his fellow countrymen, he should fulfil it because this is what the Lord requires.

The benefits of having a faithful leader are numerous. He is simply a blessing. For example, all members of the public benefit a lot when a faithful leader is in power. This is because he seeks to fulfil his promises and national obligations, which he has undertaken before during the time of swearing to fulfil before God and man. Also, by being faithful to his fellow citizens, he is indirectly teaching them to be faithful in dealing with each other, too. Also, he is ready to honour the vow that he has made to God. Because of the leader's faithfulness, the Lord will shower him and his family with blessings and elongate the period of his rule. God will also bless the whole nation because of the faithfulness of the leader. In addition, the nation will enjoy peace, good neighbourliness, economic prosperity and political stability.

A national leader's mistake is enough to bring God's curse and damnation upon a nation; whereas his faithfulness could open God's blessings upon the whole land. That is why our world pines for faithful leaders. In order for a nation to get faithful leaders, it is imperative for all its citizens to elect men and women of moral excellence to leadership positions. This is the essence of democracy, which affords all people the opportunity to participate in choosing their leaders. And if they are not to do that, who are they to blame when bad people come to power and cause bad things to happen?

A faithful leader is a real torchbearer for good governance in the executive because all his words, deeds and even thoughts are expressed in the true light of God's faithfulness. A faithless leader is actually the actual torchbearer for bad governance and corruption in the executive.

Nonetheless, the faithfulness of the president alone is insufficient in bringing about good governance within and beyond the executive without the complementary faithfulness of the cabinet members.

The Importance of the Faithfulness of the Cabinet

"Now it is required that those who have been given a trust must prove faithful" (1 Cor. 4:2). Do cabinet members owe the public any trust? Absolutely yes! As a result, they must remain faithful to their words and deeds before man and God. But do they always comply with this mandate in their pursuit of national duties?

Besides the president, the others who wield great power and social responsibility are cabinet members. Thus, if they are morally corrupt, it can be unfair for us to speak of good governance in the executive. By looking around in the whole world, one is justly and morally compelled to conclude that most of the members of the cabinets of the national governments lack divine faithfulness because they hardly fulfil their promises and national obligations.

For example, our current global cabinets are occupied by majority of faithless members. They are faithless to themselves; they are faithless to their Creator; they are faithless to their presidents, and they are faithless to fellow citizens. Their lack of faithfulness makes them vulnerable to embrace and practise some poor moral values in their daily lives. They faithlessly carry out their national duties without fulfilling the promises they made to the public. As a result, people lost faith in them. So they are leaders without followers.

In order for good governance to thrive in the executive, members of the cabinet must adopt God's faithfulness as the cornerstone of their moral values because the faithfulness of the president is not enough to bring good governance without theirs. To uphold their divine faithfulness, they must not commit themselves to do something of which they would eventually prove inept, for the Lord expects them to imitate His faithfulness. The cabinet members are to remain faithful to their words when they make them, irrespective of whether they are made to God or to man.

In the final analysis, it is good for us to understand fully that good governance is possible in the executive only when men and women working in the cabinet cherish the divine faithfulness and adopt it as the cornerstone of their ethical values by being faithful to their words, to their deeds and to their thoughts before God and man. It's also achievable in the executive when the faithful members who work in the cabinet revolutionise the entire executive by making it to uphold the divine faithfulness through which it has to discharge its national activities.

It is the moral duty of the president and other relevant agents in a given nation to play maximum care when they appoint members of the cabinet so as to get men and women who are of high moral calibre, especially those who base their personal behaviour and relationships on God's faithfulness. The appointment of faithless people into the cabinet makes the cabinet faithless, too.

Our executive branches of governments urgently require faithful cabinets to work as the actual co-torchbearers for good governance in our world. But in order to achieve really good governance in the executive, bureaucrats must also cherish God's faithfulness as the fundamental foundation on which they are to base their moral character.

Importance of the Faithfulness of Bureaucrats

It is not correct for us to speak of good governance in the executive branch of the government if the bureaucracy is made up of faithless men and women who are there to carry out the administrative tasks of the government in a faithless manner. It is also not true for any group of people to talk about an efficient and coherent bureaucracy that can help the government to carry out any major change if members of the bureaucracy do not base their own personal character on the divine faithfulness, for it is difficult to bring efficiency and coherence among faithless people. A lot of significant government programs are now failing in many parts of the world due to lack of faithful bureaucrats.

For example, when bureaucrats lack the essence of faithfulness in their lives, they also lack God in their lives. Without God's presence in their lives, they execute their national duties with no moral integrity and hence, with little success. They put their personal interest above the national interest, and because of this, people lose faith in them. They are determined to pull down their national cabinet and president from their leadership positions and thrust the nation into the deepest pit of corruption. I wonder whether you expect such faithless bureaucrats to promote good moral values and good governance in the government systems!

God expects bureaucrats to be men and women who base their personal ethical values on the divine faithfulness by being faithful, first and foremost, to themselves, by being faithful to God and by being faithful to their fellow human beings. Their faithfulness should show that they keep their promises. They cannot commit themselves to do something of which they will eventually regret and hence, prove incompetent. They are to emulate God's faithfulness, and they should not promise things thoughtlessly. But when they make promises, they must remain faithful to them in every way.

When the bureaucracy is composed of faithful people, the entire nation will experience a lot of blessings. For instance, multifaceted development will occur in all corners of the nation; the principle of equity and equality will mark the distribution of national resources and jobs allocations; the level of divine faithfulness will increase in the public, and a peaceful atmosphere will prevail within and beyond the national boundaries. Also, the Lord will continue to bless the whole nation for the greater benefit of human beings and for His own glory, too.

In conclusion, the bureaucrats become real co-torchbearers for good governance within and outside the executive branch of the government when they embrace God's faithfulness as a unique mark of their moral character and through which they are to carry out their national tasks. But this is only possible when faithfulness has saturated the whole bureaucracy, compelling it to discharge its national duties in the light of God's faithfulness. We should not just preach against corruption; the most effective way to fight corruption is by being faithful to our words and responsible for our actions.

Also, other branches of the executive such as the armed forces—the police and its paramilitary department, the army, the prison, the wildlife and game wardens—should embrace God's faithfulness to guide their values. The Lord expects all civil servants working in these important executive branches to emulate His faithfulness as the basis upon which they are to base their ethical behaviour. He wants them to prove true and keep their promises under all circumstances. Since they have taken an oath to execute national obligations, they are not to give their words and not to follow through with their promises.

It is the collective duty of the top leadership of the executive, the legislature and the judiciary to choose morally right people, especially those who base their ethical character and personal relationships on God's faithfulness, to serve as civil servants in the bureaucracy and all other law-enforcement agencies. Thus, when all these branches do their national work in the light of God's faithfulness, we can say with full confidence that good governance exists in and outside the executive branch of the government.

In summary, good governance is only possible in the executive when the president, the cabinet and bureaucrats, among others, embrace the divine faithfulness in its totality as the basic foundation upon which to establish their personal code of conduct and through which to carry out their day-to-day national obligations. Also, when their faithfulness has completely pervaded the entire executive system, we can then comfortably speak of all members of the executive as being the actual torchbearers for good governance within and without the executive. In a nutshell, good governance is possible in the executive only when all its workers embrace and practise genuineness, veracity and faithfulness in their day-to-day activities.

Let's now explore divine love and its role in changing the minds and hearts of the workers in the executive so as to bring about the existence of real good governance. The four elements of love that will guide our discussion are benevolence, grace, mercy and persistence.

Chapter 3
Love in the Executive

There is consensus that love is the basic moral attribute of God; it defines the very nature of God. And those who believe this have biblical backing because Apostle John in his letter says: "Whoever does not love does not know God, because God is love. And so we know and rely on the love God has for us. God is love. Whoever lives in love lives in God, and God in him" (1 Jn. 4:8, 16).

God's love is best portrayed by His provision to His creation and His giving of Himself. In exploring the importance of God's love in delivering good governance in the executive organ of the government, it will help if we begin by yielding our minds, hearts, souls and spirits once more to this divine attribute as urged by our Lord and Saviour Jesus Christ: "… Love the Lord your God with all your heart and with all your soul and with all your mind… love your neighbour as yourself" (Matt. 22:37-40).

Today, out of pride, some government officials, including heads of state, do not acknowledge the existence of God and that He is the Creator of the universe. And even the love for God for many who believe in His existence does not go beyond the occasional mention of His name in their discussion. Yet the Bible requires that they love Him with all their hearts and with all their souls and with all their minds. And there is no better way to demonstrate this than to yield their conduct to His guidance. What then is the real object of the love of those who do not believe in the existence of God? The object of their love can only be themselves.

However, it is good for me to acknowledge that despite the carnality and atheism prevalent among most of the government officials in different parts of entire world, there are still some real believers who wholeheartedly love the Lord their God with all their hearts and with all their souls and with all their minds. These real believers are the actual salt and the light of the world. One of such few God-fearing leaders is the late Rev. Dr. Martin Luther King, Jr.

Just as they do not have love for God—seeing they do not know Him (1Jn. 4:16)—atheists do not genuinely love their fellow human beings. Those who live in love live in God and God lives in them (1 Jn. 4:16). Atheists may demonstrate some form of love (usually erotic or sensual) to their fellow human beings, but it is hard, if not totally impossible, for them to realize the essence of the second greatest commandment, which says, "Love your neighbour as yourself" (Matt. 22:39). Our love for others emanates from our pure love for our Creator; actually, our love for others is basically His love radiating from us to others. So, if we do not honestly love the Lord, it is impossible to talk of loving others genuinely.

In the same way, carnal believers may demonstrate some sort of love for their fellow human beings, but it is not true love because they are not deeply immersed in the divine love of God. It is when we are fully immersed in divine love that we radiate the same quality of love to others.

According to MacArthur, "Biblical love meets people's

needs."[8] If we sincerely love our neighbours as we love ourselves, the whole world will have been divested of corruption and other malpractices that result in so much suffering. For instance, if we love our neighbours as we love ourselves, we will honour our fathers and mothers so that we may live long in this world. Also, evils like murder, adultery, theft and giving of false testimony against neighbours will be non-existent. Nor will anyone see the point of coveting their neighbour's household or covet their neighbour's wife or husband, their maidservant or manservant, their oxen or donkeys or anything that belongs to their neighbour (Exod. 20:12-17). One may think that it is impossible for human beings to attain this level of love, but this is what our loving Lord requires of us, and He would not have demanded what He knows is outside our ability.

Just to be honest with ourselves and with God, corruption is not external but internal; it pervades deep down in our system. It is a form of sin which is deeply rooted within our own lives. It is a manifestation of the absence of God's love in human life, the result of moral decay. If we want to eradicate corruption and malpractices from our own lives and our nations, the most effective way is to start fighting them from within. Jesus says, "For out of the heart come evil thoughts, murder, adultery, sexual immorality, theft, false testimony, slander. These are what make a man 'unclean'; but eating with unwashed hands does not make him 'unclean'" (Matt. 15:19a). It is an undeniable fact that human corruption or uncleanness is from within, not from without.

Having established the centrality of love in the nature of God as well as in the life of man, the image of God, I will now discuss how the four facets of love—benevolence, grace, mercy, persistence—can advance good governance in the executive

8   MacArthur, John. The Master's Plan for the Church. Chicago: Moody Press, 1991.

part of the government when all the workers sincerely repent of their known and unknown sins and totally embrace divine love as the cornerstone of their moral character and the yardstick with which they are to discharge their national obligations.

Benevolence

Benevolence is an act of charity and kindness. Some of its identical terms are kindness, compassion, generosity and goodwill. It is best demonstrated through the concern of the Lord for the welfare of those whom He loves. God sacrificially seeks out for people. For instance, in John 3:16 it is written, 'For God so loved the world that he gave his one and only Son, that whoever believes in him shall not perish but have eternal life.'

According to Richard Kriegbaum, "No one should support or follow a leader who does not truly love him. No one should attempt to lead people he does not care about."[10] It is worth gleaning and bathing ourselves in such wisdom. As you follow me in this discussion on the role of God's love in the attainment of good governance in the executive, you will realize that it is important for all the personnel in the executive—the president, members of the cabinet, bureaucrats, etc. —to sincerely love and care for their followers if they want them to love and follow them in return.

In this section, let us explore the possibility of realizing good governance in the executive by having the conduct of the president, cabinet members, bureaucrats, etc. guided by divine benevolence.

Vitality of the Benevolence of a President

The president is an important person, the rallying point of the entire nation. He is the one who holds the leadership torch as

---

10 Ibid., Kriegbaum, 117.

the nation strives towards its vision and mission. It is therefore, easy to see the tragedy that can result from his being morally corrupt: he would lead the whole nation astray, thrusting it into the abyss of moral decay. The president who does not base his personal character and social relationships on God's benevolence does not demonstrate love, for there is no true love without God, and by living and working without God, he exposes himself to all forces of evil, hating others and being hated by them in return. Eventually, he loses all types of support from his family members, his cabinet and other civil servants. And not just that, as the leader of a rebellious team, lot of his time that should go towards planning and implementing policy is taken up by unhealthy scheming for the downfall of 'dangerous' followers. But what he fails to understand is that the more of his followers fall, the more his power is undermined because they are the ones propping him up on their painful shoulders.

This kind of president has no good moral values. Hence, he is not morally equipped to lead his nation towards their realization of the fruit of the Spirit so that citizens can enjoy love, joy, peace, patience, kindness, faithfulness, goodness, gentleness and self- control (Gal. 5:22-23a). Instead, he leads his nation in yielding to the sinful nature by defiling themselves with all manner of acts of the flesh like sexual immorality, impurity and debauchery, idolatry and witchcraft, hatred, discord, jealousy, fits of rage, selfish ambition, dissensions, factions and envy, drunkenness, orgies, and the like (Gal. 5:19b-21a). Surely, can such a president be the torchbearer for good governance in any nation?

The state leader should be the torchbearer for good governance in the executive. God expects him to emulate the divine benevolence to guide his character as he addresses leadership issues in God's name. He should take care of the welfare of those whom he loves and leads by seeking their interests unselfishly. A leader should not be vengeful as he interacts with the members of his public; instead, he should imitate God's benevolence by showing kindness to both his friends and foes, for Jesus Christ says you must love your enemies and pray for those who persecute or maltreat you so "that you may be sons of your Father in heaven. He causes his sun to rise on the evil and the good, and sends rain on the righteous and the unrighteous" (Matt. 5:45).

The benevolence of the state leader should not be limited to his fellow human beings; it should extend to other creatures of God, such as animals, birds, fish, et cetera. This is in line with God's original edict: "… Rule over the fish of the sea and the birds of the air and over every living creature that moves on the ground" (Gen. 1:28b). The fish, the birds and other creatures benefit a lot from good governance. Hence, the president has some executive powers and responsibility to safeguard the existence of such vulnerable but beautiful creatures for God's glory. This too has biblical backing. Jesus said:

> Look at the birds of the air; they do not sow or reap or store away in barns, and yet your heavenly Father feeds them... See how the lilies of the field grow. They do not labor or spin. Yet I tell you that not even Solomon in all his splendour was dressed like one of these (Matt. 6:26a, 28-29).

It is therefore, clear why the president should defend all creatures and lovingly protect their habitat.

The president as the torchbearer for good governance in and outside the executive should not only empathise with the objects of his love but also act to protect their general wellbeing. By being kind to all his subjects, including the subhuman creatures, his benevolence will, in return, endear him to the wider public. Moreover, members of the public will emulate his benevolence and practise it among themselves, resulting in a loving and peaceful atmosphere and general prosperity within and outside the national borders. Eventually, his enemies will change to friends. All the other creatures will enjoy unprecedented tranquillity, thus, attracting the blessings of the Almighty God to the entire nation.

But when the wider public is afraid of their leader, he ceases to be their leader and becomes their enemy instead. People should not fear but, instead, respect their leader.

A benevolent leader is a qualified torchbearer for good governance in the executive. Take away divine benevolence and you will remain with what is just love by name. Our world is longing for kind leaders whose moral values are characterized by God's benevolence, people intent on leading their nations along the path of God's love. Only then can we justifiably speak of such leaders as the real torchbearers for good governance in the executives. And for us to have such leaders wielding authority in our midst, all registered voters in the nations should exercise their national duty by voting to power men and women of high ethical standing, especially those known for having the divine benevolence in their lives, to steer the nations along the path of good morals and hence, good governance.

But the benevolence of the president alone is not sufficient for the realization of good governance; the complementary benevolence of his cabinet is equally necessary.

Importance of the Benevolence of Cabinet

In any government, the cabinet holds an important position within the executive because its members are the key people heading different intra-governmental agencies. A strong cabinet produces a strong government and vice versa. This is because the executive president relies heavily on his cabinet to carry out his national duties.

When members of the cabinet fail to base their conduct and social relationships on God's benevolence, they carry out their national duties and relate to one another, to their president and to other members of the public in unloving manner. Thus, the loving Lord will not find a worthy place in their lives. Hence, they will operate and live without him. In the absence of God and His love in their lives, members of the cabinet put their personal interests above the national interests because of the diminished love for their fellow countrymen. They do not love them as they love themselves. And as they continue to pursue their individual goals at the expense of the welfare of the general public, they spoil the leadership of the president and thus, undermine his authority in the process.

Without the actual spirit of the divine benevolence in them, they lack the courage to advocate for moral values and courage to promote good governance in and outside the executive. And unless measures are taken in time, such a cabinet could lure the bureaucrats and other government officials into immorality and bring the entire nation to her knees.

What are God's expectations from the cabinet in regard to His benevolence? God expects men and women working in the cabinet to embrace His kind of benevolence as the guiding principle of their moral values. This divine benevolence will enable them to wholeheartedly and unselfishly seek the general welfare of the members of the public. Also, they are to show their benevolence to their enemies because they are fellow countrymen who also participated in giving the cabinet its mandate. And this is also in accordance with God's word, for Paul urges: "Be kind and compassionate to one another, forgiving each other, just as in Christ God forgave you" (Eph. 4:32).

We very well know, of course, that two wrongs do not make a single right; therefore, leaders should not hit back at those who hate them. Through their benevolence, cabinet members are expected to take care of the environment, including animals and their habitat, for this is in line with God's will. Both the members of the public and other subhuman creatures are like frail children who need tender care from adults. For this reason, unkind people are unfit for positions in the cabinet. Their kind of important work requires compassionate men and women so that their kindness can make the entire executive conducive for good governance.

Cabinet members can only become the real co-torchbearers for good governance in the executive when they portray their actual benevolence both in private and in public. They should also join hands with the president and use their clout to bring all the corners of the executive and the entire government to the divine light of benevolence. Better still, they should do all the work that they are mandated to do in the light of God's benevolence.

In order to get these unique people from among members of the public, the president plus the others concerned should sincerely and lovingly appoint persons of noble virtues, particularly God's benevolence, to occupy positions in the cabinet.

But the benevolence of the president and that of his cabinet alone is not sufficient for good governance in the executive. The benevolence of the entire bureaucracy is also required. The following section explores how bureaucrats can become co-torchbearers for good governance by embracing God's benevolence.

Importance of the Benevolence of Bureaucrats

When men and women working in the bureaucracy are unkind to their seniors as well as the general public, they will not be able to do a good job. If this continues, it may eventually disqualify them from being the real co-torchbearers for good governance in the executive. Bureaucrats who lack the essence of divine benevolence in their character are torchbearers for national disaster, not good governance.

Many executive organs worldwide are currently manned by bureaucrats who lack God's benevolence. This is a reflection of their deficiency of the true love and love of God in their lives. As a result, they have attracted God's anger upon themselves as well as upon their nations. Their unkind words and deeds have not been in keeping with the people's aspirations, for it is always difficult, if not totally impossible, to give good services to people whom you don't love. Genuine benevolence is what compels you to serve them as well as you would want to be served yourself.

Unkind bureaucrats put their narrow interests above national goals. They treat members of the public unkindly. As a result, they trigger ill feelings from the public. If the president and the cabinet base their conduct and personal relationships on God's benevolence, they don't support the behaviour of unkind bureaucrats. And this automatically leads to unhealthy tension between these vital organs of the executive. With the resulting disharmony and disunity within the executive, the whole nation is unable to realize her set vision.

Therefore, for the bureaucrats to achieve high credibility in carrying out their executive duties, God expects them to embrace His benevolence as the guide to their moral conduct. This will lovingly guide them as they relate to themselves, as they relate to their Creator and as they relate to and interact with their fellow human beings. Benevolence ought to make the bureaucrats concerned about the welfare of the general public. In fact, they should be the civil servants who have both social and religious responsibilities to serve the Lord by serving their people wholeheartedly. They are not just to serve those who love them but also to serve their enemies because the benevolent God whom they fashion their lives after is good to all, making the sun to shine on both the evil and on the good people and sending rain on the just and on the unjust (Matt. 5:45).

Bureaucrats are to show their divine benevolence to subhuman creatures as well. This is the way God does things, for the Bible in Psalm 145:16 says, "You open your hand and satisfy the desires of every living thing." Our Lord Jesus corroborate what the Psalmist says by explaining that the Father cares for the birds of the air and the lilies of the field in terms of their feeding and clothing (Matt. 6:26, 28). Not a single sparrow falls down without God noticing (Matt. 10:29). The bureaucrats are not under obligation to have certain feelings of love towards the objects of their benevolence; all that is required of them is to act in their best interest.

When the bureaucrats demonstrate divine benevolence in their relationships with their Creator as well as in their relationships with their fellow human beings, the Lord is pleased with them, and so is the entire nation. As a result, He will bestow His sincere blessings on the whole nation, including all the subhuman creatures, making the entire land experiences peace, love, good neighbourliness and general prosperity. Our world pines for bureaucrats who by embracing God's benevolence shine as the true co-torchbearers for good governance within and beyond the executive.

I can authoritatively summarize here that the bureaucrats can become the real co-torchbearers for good governance only when they base their ethical values on God's benevolence. In fact, good governance requires that divine benevolence saturates the whole executive to enable officials discharge their work responsibly.

In addition, it is important for all the other departments of the executive, like the armed forces, to embrace God's benevolence as a mark of their ethical behaviour. Moreover, it should become part of their daily lives as they relate with their fellow countrymen and in the course of carrying out their national duties. We cannot truly speak of the presence of good governance within the executive and the entire Government if some of the important organs lack God's benevolence. If we want to see true good governance in the executive, all the organs involved must join hands in collectively living out divine benevolence and making it their guiding principle in discharging their duties. Of course, in order to achieve this, those responsible for filling important positions in the civil service should be people of high integrity, known particularly for God's benevolence.

In summary, good governance in the executive is only possible so long as the president, the cabinet and bureaucracy, among others, are guided by God's benevolence. It is only when the right moral values inform the basic policies and principles by which the executive operates can we talk of having good governance in the executive.

To fight the rampant corruption and other anomalies or evils in our national governments, we have to start with ourselves before pointing out the mistakes of others. However, in order to realize truly good governance in the executive in the light of God's love, let us now consider the role of divine grace, the second facet of love.

Grace

Grace is the other important component of divine love. From a Christian perspective, grace means the unmerited favour of God, that is, goodwill. God deals with his people not in line with their merit but merely in accordance with their needs

- he deals with them according to his goodness and generosity towards them.

When members of the executive deal with one another as well as with the general public without God's grace, their interactions lack a significant ingredient of God's love. The result is a clear moral defect in their conduct and in carrying out national tasks.

Let us now explore the role of God's grace in the personnel working in different sectors of the executive and its contribution towards good governance, beginning with the president.

Importance of the Grace in a President

If the president is not driven by God's grace to become the torchbearer for good governance in the executive and the government as a whole, who can it be? The president is the one to champion the fight against corruption and other evils, or else he becomes the actual torchbearer for bad governance, guided by Satan's vindictiveness.

A president who lacks God's grace lacks love because he is without God, the source of genuine love. Consequently, such a leader becomes an abode for the implacable, vengeful Satan. His union with the evil forces allows him to deal and interrelate with his cabinet and other officials in a tyrannical way. Ruthlessness characterizes his moral conduct, and makes the general public fear and distant themselves from him.

Such a cruel president is like a hurricane that destroys all the weak and leaves only the strong. Unfortunately, we sometimes see and hear the exodus of frighten people fleeing from their own homelands and seeking refuge in foreign lands due to the gracelessness of their state rulers. Starting right from his office, the working environment that such a leader creates is tense, and hence, people feel less comfortable to work there. Lack of divine grace in his professionalism and vast experience makes him "only a resounding gong or a clanging cymbal" (1Cor. 13:1b). He has no good moral values to enhance his leadership. This makes him far from being the torchbearer for good governance within and outside the executive.

Apostle Paul says, "For it is by grace you have been saved, through faith—and this is not from yourselves, it is the gift of God—not by works, so that no one can boast" (Eph. 2:8-9). This is the same saving grace that the gracious God wants a leader to extend to all his subjects, knowing very well that "...all have sinned and fall short of the glory of God, and are justified freely by his grace through the redemption that came by Christ Jesus" (Rom. 3:23-24). A gracious leader deals with his people, including his political opponents and other enemies, in a charitable manner. And when he must take action, he does it through the just national law rather than taking the law into his own hand and dealing ruthlessly with those he doesn't like. Whenever a gracious leader is on the throne, his people rejoice and deal with him graciously. He is well aware that he too has sinned and fallen short of the glory of God (Rom. 3:23).

In order for the state leader to shine as a real torchbearer for good governance, God expects him to adopt the divine grace as a recognisable mark of his moral character and efficient and effective apparatus with which he is to carry out his presidential duties. As a gracious leader, he must deal with his people, not on the basis of their worthiness, but according to their needs. His goodness compels him to work towards the general aspirations of his subjects, whether they love him or not. Through divine grace, he forgives the members of his public who have wronged him. He is worthy vessel through which God's grace is conveyed to other living things.

The gracious leader affords all members of the public the right to enjoy what they earn with their sweat without fearing undue or due reprisal from the throne. They view their president as a facilitator of life, not of death. Unfortunately, some leaders play unhealthy tit-for-tat games like small children. Above all, graciousness on the part of the leader is a pre-condition for God's blessings on the nation. A gracious leader attracts blessings from God.

The president becomes a real torchbearer for good governance only when he embraces the divine grace as the guide for his moral values in carrying out his executive tasks in the light of God's grace. Our world is thirsting for gracious leaders to rule and lead their people according to God's will. Therefore, it is the primary role of the people to elect godly people, gracious men and women, to lead them.

But in order for the president's grace to bring about sustainable good governance in the executive, there is need for the members of the cabinet to also be co-torchbearers for good governance in the executive in the light of God's grace. Hence, this is the focus of the following section.

Importance of Grace in the Cabinet

Members of the cabinet have the critical role of upholding the president and his government. So their weakness or strength determines the fate of the government and its president. When the cabinet is strong, so is the president, making it easy for his government to rule with ease. A weak cabinet, on the other hand, makes even the strongest leader weak and brings his government down on its knees. Thus, for the president to enjoy an enabling environment in which good governance thrives in the executive, he must have the backing of a strong cabinet that is made up of gracious people.

When members of the cabinet lack God's grace in their personal lives, they lack in themselves real love and God, the actual source of the divine love. As a result, they become the very slaves of the evil forces. They relate to their president and other members of the public in a hostile manner, though they would love that people deal with them mercifully when they go wrong. Unfortunately, their ungracious attitude towards people has the undesirable effect of engendering animosity between them and common people. Also, their behaviour does not promote ethical norms and good governance in the executive, for these do not exist where divine love is absent.

To reverse or, better still, pre-empt this toxic leadership situation, God expects all the cabinet members to embrace His divine grace as the actual basis of their moral character. It should be the one by which they relate among themselves, deal with the general public and commune with their Lord. In the course of their work, they are to deal with people, not on the basis of their financial worth or standing in society but in accordance with their needs. People are after a cabinet that is capable of addressing their needs graciously.

The cabinet members become true co-torchbearers for good governance only when the divine grace is the foundation of their ethical values and the guide for carrying out their executive responsibilities. Nobody wants ruthless cabinet members entrusted with matters of national interest. Thus, the president, the legislature and the judiciary should exercise prudence, guided by high moral values, when appointing members of the cabinet. This will enable them man this vital organ of the government with gracious men and women.

But it is quite obvious that despite the divine grace of both the president and his cabinet, good governance in the executive would still not be possible in the absence of God's grace in the bureaucracy.

Importance of Gracious Bureaucrats

When this huge group of government personnel is not refined morally, the government is exposed to ethical collapse. Unless the bureaucracy bases itself on God's grace, it is impossible (or just a mere dream) to expect good governance in and outside the executive, even if other civil servants are morally good.

Graceless bureaucrats act and relate to one another without love. They interact with members of the cabinet and the president without love. And they serve the general public ruthlessly, being the wrong people in important places. They place their personal goals above national interests. In the course of their work, they leave a trail of destruction, creating enmity with their bosses and the members of the public whom they are supposed to serve. As it is not always possible to serve people you don't love, the performance of such bureaucrats is dismal, characterized more by serving selfish interests and eventually leading the nation towards hatred, jealousy, envy and disunity. Indeed, what else can a ruthless bureaucracy bestow upon its nation and mankind in general?

In order for bureaucrats to act as true co-torchbearers for good governance in the executive, the Lord expects them to embrace His divine grace as the recognisable trademark of their conduct as they discharge their national duties. In the course of their work, they should not deal with people on the basis of their merit but mercifully according to their personal needs. This is because if the bureaucrats carry out their national duties on the basis of people's worth, they may end up serving just a small section of the entire population, for people, especially non-Christians, are sinful.

Furthermore, the bureaucrats become real co-torchbearers for good governance in the executive only if they fully embrace the divine grace as a true mark of their ethical character and use it as the clear light through which they carry out their executive duties. The Lord put them there to graciously serve Him by serving His people, guided by divine grace.

When the gracious bureaucrats deal with their fellow human beings and carry out their national tasks in the light of the divine grace, brotherhood, peace, good neighbourliness and general prosperity will increase in and beyond the nation. The whole nation receives God's abundant blessings in return. Our Lord requires gracious men and women to work in the government bureaucracy for the common benefit of mankind and for His own glory.

However, for us to realize proper good governance in the executive branch of the government, other sectors of the executive—for instance, the armed forces—must also adopt God's grace as the basis of their conduct. Divine grace will enable them discharge their national duties, not according to the merit of the members of the public but on the basis of people's needs. It is mandatory for them to deal with their people in the light of God's grace. But in order to improve on our bureaucracy and the armed forces, the recruiting agents should be transparent and accountable enough in the way they exercise this vital function so as to put people whose conduct is ethically sound in the right places. We shouldn't just employ hostile people and hope that things will be fine in the government and the whole nation!

In conclusion, good governance is only possible when all the sectors of the executive—the president, the cabinet, the bureaucracy, et cetera—embrace God's grace as the benchmark of moral values which are to guide them in discharging their national duties.

But for real good governance to exist in the executive, let us explore how the mercy of the president, cabinet, bureaucrats and other agents in the executive branch of the government promote the existence of good governance in and outside the executive.

Mercy

From the general usage, 'mercy' means 'compassion' or 'forbearance' towards defeated enemies or offenders. And from a biblical viewpoint, 'mercy' refers to the kindness of God in withholding deserved judgement and extending undeserved compassion and forgiveness to man. Moreover, God is able to do this without compromising His justice as seen in the very death and resurrection of Jesus Christ in the place of sinners. Mercy is a Christian virtue that all believers are required to show.

As we know, the executive branch of the government consists of the president, the cabinet, bureaucracy, et cetera. In the next section, we explore the role of mercy in the performance of executive president, in the lives and performance of the cabinet members, in the lives of the bureaucrats as well as in the lives and performance of the armed forces with the ultimate aim of realizing good governance.

Importance of Mercy in a President

It is worth mentioning here that any leader is in charge of people of different calibre, different interests and varied characteristics. Some people have refined moral values, while others are ethically below standard. And not just that, some fellow countrymen under him may be very difficult to deal with. Needless to say, there are good and bad citizens in any given population. Yet all of them belong to the Lord, who would like their leader to lead them well. To fulfil God's will under such circumstances, the leader should make divine mercy as the cornerstone of his moral character because without such mercy, he will end up wiping out the troublesome citizens.

But some nations have not been blessed with merciful leaders who are in a position to lead people in godly ways. Instead, such leaders inflict unbearable sufferings on them. Some presidents are devoid of God and hence, without love, the real source of divine mercy. These merciless leaders are common in the Third World countries where people live and die under some form of the law of the jungle.

Without God's mercy in his own life, the president lives and governs his people in constant fear. This is because his merciless leadership causes him to have numerous enemies. As a result, he is afraid of his own life and well aware that others may harm him as they seek revenge. Yet others, especially his subordinates and other government officials, fear him greatly. Such a leader lacks good moral values to offer his countrymen and the rest of the mankind.

It is good for us to know that "God's mercy is his tender-hearted, loving compassion for his people. It is his tenderness of heart toward the needy. If grace contemplates man as sinful, guilty, and condemned, mercy sees him as miserable and needy."[11] As a result, for the president to shine as a torchbearer for good governance, guided by God's mercy, he should embrace God's mercy as the yardstick of his ethical character. Then with this divine character, he will deal tenderly with his people and demonstrate loving compassion for his people. He is to show pity on them at all times and not view them as a source of his problems but as sheep deserving a shepherd. Such were the helpless people whom Jesus saw in His day as recorded in the book of Matthew:

> Jesus went through all the towns and villages, teaching in their synagogues, preaching the good news of the kingdom and healing every disease and sickness. When

---

11 Ibid., Erickson, 295.

he saw the crowds, he had compassion on them, because they were harassed and helpless, like sheep without a shepherd (Matt. 9:35-36).

Therefore, for the president to become a worthy torchbearer for good governance in the executive in the light of God's mercy, he should holistically care for his people by exemplifying himself as a good shepherd. His mercy should show his tenderness and compassion for his people.

But to have such dignified and merciful leaders in power, it is our collective duty globally to exercise our democratic right by choosing persons of high ethical values, particularly God's mercy, as national presidents. If we elect merciless leaders, we will naturally reap what we plant!

However, for the executive to experience sound governance that is guided by God's mercy, members of the cabinet must also be good co-torchbearers for good governance in the executive branches of the government.

Importance of the Mercy among Cabinet Members

Very often, some of these leaders are not concerned about the welfare of the general public. Instead, they mind only their own affairs and leave a majority of their fellow countrymen languishing in slums under deplorable conditions. Yet such poor people are the voters who put the merciless cabinet members in power and shoulder the dehumanizing policies the latter come up with. And if these poor people remain in the slums without the attention of their government's representatives, a time comes when they get fed up and take the bull by the horn by hurling them down from their shoulders.

When members of the cabinet lack God's mercy in their own lives, they are ruthless in the way they discharge their duties and in the social relationships as well. First, they become merciless towards one another, towards their national president and towards other citizens. Their inhumane behaviour makes the general public lose faith in them, and they in turn respond by being hostile towards them. Similarly, their president may become hard in dealing with, particularly when they make mistakes. As a result, their social relationships and carrying out of national duties are undermined by the tension that the ensuing hatred, discord, jealousy, envy and disunity bring about. In fact, a ruthless cabinet lacks God and hence, His love in it. As such, it has no moral values to offer to its nation and outsiders.

Therefore, in order for the cabinet members to qualify as co-torchbearers for good governance in the executive, they must adopt God's mercy as the concrete benchmark of their moral values. Jesus ordered His followers, "Be merciful, just as your Father is merciful" (Lk. 6:36). Of course, if they deal mercifully with their fellow citizens, He will in turn deal with them with understanding. When divine mercy is domiciled in their lives, cabinet members consider the suffering or the rejoicing of their people as their own. They feel hurt when people hurt and enjoy when their people are happy. This is the state of affairs that our world pines for, where members of the cabinet demonstrate divine mercy as the trademark of their ethical character as well as the recognisable standard of their leadership.

Our presidents, the legislatures and the judiciaries should exercise prudence when appointing members of the cabinet so as to choose people who are known for being ethical, especially those who exhibit God's mercy. Wrong choices always lead to trouble unless God intervenes.

We can speak of the members of the cabinet as co-torchbearers for good governance in the executive only when they put on the mantle of divine mercy as the basic standard of their moral values. Guided by their divine character, cabinet members deal tenderly with and show loving compassion to their people by rejoicing with them when they are rejoicing and mourning with them when they are mourning. God and men are happy with this kind of rulers, and under such a state of affairs, one can comfortably speak of the existence of good governance in the nation.

But in order for us to realise truly good governance in the executive, the entire bureaucracy should also embrace God's mercy and thus, engender an enabling environment for general operations.

Importance of the Mercy in the Bureaucracy

Given their great number, if bureaucrats deal ruthlessly with their people, especially the majority poor, the masses will suffer very much under such a government. Under such circumstances, bureaucrats become torchbearers for bad instead of good governance. To illustrate this viewpoint, when majority of the bureaucrats do not base their ethical behaviours and social and business relationships on God's mercy, they interact and deal with the people, including the president and his cabinet in a ruthless manner. They put their own selfish goals above people's interests. They don't see people, especially the common man, through the eyes of the merciful Lord. As a result, their ruthless behaviour makes them unsuitable civil servants and hence, enemies of the people. Without God's love in them, they have no useful ethical norms to guide their own code of conduct, to guide the way they discharge their duties, or to teach their people and other human beings. Ruthless bureaucrats are not good promoters of good governance in and outside the executive.

Therefore, for there to be proper governance in the executive, it is imperative for all members of the bureaucracy to embrace the divine mercy as the true mark of their ethical character and use it to saturate and turn the entire bureaucracy into an oasis of God's mercy. Practising divine mercy will make them interact with their people tenderly, portraying their compassion for them. They must see them as people who deserve their genuine sympathy because most of the members of the public live in deplorable socio-economic and political situations.

People are inherently depraved, and our bureaucracies in the entire world are thirsting for sincere and merciful people to man them. These are people who will deal with the masses with understanding. People need underserved mercy from their own leaders. Like God who has shown His divine mercy to mankind regardless of their moral character, bureaucrats too are expected to extend this divine mercy to their fellow human beings, irrespective of their moral quality.

Bureaucrats become the actual co-torchbearers for good governance in the executive only when they firmly embrace God's mercy as the basic yardstick of their ethical values and use it as the lenses through which they view their people when they deal with them on a day-to-day basis. When they show mercy in their relationship with the general public, the general public responds by being merciful to them. Also, it is only when the whole bureaucracy becomes a pool of the divine mercy in which members of the general public swim and quench their thirst can we correctly speak of the bureaucrats as the real co-torchbearers for good governance in the executive in the light of God's mercy.

However, for good governance to abound in the executive branch of the government, all the armed forces must also embrace the divine mercy as a guide to their policies as they deal with people. In the course of their work, they are to be tender towards the citizens, and their compassionate actions towards them should be loud and clear. For instance, when police and prison deal with some members of the public who have broken the law, they are to show their loving compassion for them because the general intent of the law is not to kill people but to mould their crooked moral character and eventually restore them to their rightful place in society. If you need others, and especially God, to deal with you mercifully when you are wrong, you too must deal with others mercifully!

In order for us to experience the essence of God's mercy in our bureaucracies and all armed forces, those bodies entrusted with appointments to senior positions should shun any sorts of moral corruption so as to avoid choosing and putting in positions of power people with unethical character. Like God, those who lead and serve people should be merciful.

In conclusion, good governance in the executive is only feasible when the president, the cabinet and the entire bureaucracy, among others, fully embrace the divine mercy as the benchmark for their moral values and which is to guide in crafting policies and procedures of operation. It is also when this divine mercy overflows from the executive to other corners of the government that we can conclude that good governance exists in the executive.

Nevertheless, it is also good for us to understand that despite the adoption of divine mercy by the entire executive system, the essence of good governance in the executive will not exist without godly persistence in the executive being embraced by all the relevant personnel—the president, the cabinet, the bureaucrats, etc.

Persistence

Generally, the word 'persistence' refers to the act of continuing firmly or obstinately in one's opinion or action despite a series of obstacles, remonstrance, etc. But as used in this book, persistence is a final dimension of the love of the Lord. The persistence of God is portrayed in various parts of the Scriptures, such as Ps. 86:15, Rom. 2: 4, 1 Pet. 3:20 and 2 Pet. 3:15. These verses portray God as withholding judgement and continuing to offer salvation and grace over a long period of time to an unworthy people. God's persistence was apparent in God's dealing with Israel, demonstrating an outflow of His faithfulness to them. Although the Jews continually rebelled against Jehovah, at some point even desiring to return to Egypt and setting up idols for worship, and so on and so forth, the Lord did not abandon them.

But apart from the long-suffering that God demonstrated when dealing with the Israelites in the wilderness, according to Apostle Peter, God in Noah's time delayed the onset of the flood to provide the people an opportunity to repent and be saved (1 Pet. 3: 20). Also about the future day of the great judgement, Peter suggests that the second coming of Christ is delayed due to God's forbearance, for it is written: "The Lord is not slow in keeping his promise, as some understand slowness. He is patient with you, not wanting anyone to perish, but everyone to come to repentance" (2 Pet. 3: 9).

A good leader does not use his position to destroy his rebellious subjects but to give them the opportunity to reform and save them in the process, and this is the spirit that produces good governance. All government policies and procedures should be guided by godly persistence for there to be good governance in the executive. A worthy executive branch is the one that has embraced the kind of persistence that is evident in the way God deals with people. This extraordinary form of persistence is necessary in every situation that involves dealing with human beings. Any impatient employee in the executive organ is, accordingly, a ruthless one.

Let us now explore the role of persistence in good governance in the executive when it is embraced by the main departments of the executive, which include the office of the president, the cabinet and the bureaucracy.

Importance of the Persistence of a President

A president who lacks divine persistence in his own life is a leader who does not base his conduct on the sure ground of God's love. He also lacks the loving Lord in his life, for God is love. As a result, such a president makes and implements decisions hastily, only to regret later. He does not pause and think critically through the issues facing the nation so as to make prudent decisions. Instead, he moves impatiently, makes numerous mistakes and finally bears and shames himself and his nation with some silly apologies. In some cases, such mistakes could lead to the loss of good government officials and the backing of most of his followers. Unless God intervenes in his life, the impatient president's future is threatened if he continues with his hasty decisions that are not well thought out, and likewise, the future of his nation becomes uncertain.

In order for the executive president to be the real torchbearer for good governance in the executive, he must adopt God's persistence as the benchmark of his moral character and transparent lenses through which he views his presidential tasks. Leadership really requires divine persistence as the leader follows in the footsteps of God.

Since persistence is one of the components of divine love, every leader should wear it as his best necklace, showing his continuous love for his people, whether they love him or not. The requirement to forgive a brother who sins against you 490 times (Matt. 18:21-22) shows the patience that is expected of a follower of the Lord. Of course, the Lord is not saying that you should keep a record of your brother's sins against you; instead,

He is demanding that you continue forgiving him as long as he is willing to own up to his mistakes.

Just as God dealt patiently with certain biblical leaders like Moses, David and Solomon who had sinned and failed him, a real leader should not have a tit-for-tat attitude. Instead, he should patiently deal with his subjects daily, hoping that they will eventually reform and become good, loving citizens. Consequently, the more the leader deals patiently with his people, the more they also deal with him patiently.

If we want to have patient leaders in our world, we must elect men and women of high moral character, especially those who undeniably demonstrate godly persistence. Leading people calls for a high level of patience. If we choose impatient leaders to lead us, we must be fully prepared for a rough ride and keep hoping—sometimes against hope!—to reach our final destination safely.

In conclusion, for any president to be a worthy torchbearer for good governance in the executive branch of the government, he should uphold God's persistence as a recognisable mark of his moral values and saturate the entire executive system with this virtue by dealing with his people patiently and carrying out his presidential duties persistently on a daily basis. By being persistent with his people, he is in a way teaching them to be patient with him and with each other also.

Our world badly needs persistent leaders to patiently lead their fellow human beings, including those who are impatient. But we cannot talk of the spirit of real good governance in the executive in the light of God's persistence if members of the cabinet do not also act as the actual co-torchbearers for good governance in the executive in the light of God's persistence.

Importance of the Persistence of Cabinet

A cabinet that is made up of impatient members is a team the president cannot rely on. It is the bestowal of hatred, disunity and selfishness to the nation, a living temple of the evil forces. A cabinet of impatient members lacks persistence in itself, provides no room for the president to make mistakes as he exercises his leadership. Such a cabinet is also impatient with the national bureaucracy and other citizens as they do their daily work. The working environment of the cabinet is quite tense and somewhat chaotic because people don't see each other through the patient eyes of the Lord. They easily vent anger and are critical of each other. This judgemental attitude leads them to make unjustified, negative criticism among themselves, against their leader and against other members of the public. Such cabinet members have no proper moral values as a legacy to their nation and other human beings.

Hence, in order for us to realise good governance in the executive branch of the government, all cabinet members must embrace God's persistence as a clear benchmark of their ethical code of conduct and as a guide in their day-to-day activities. This is because a persistent president who lacks a persistent cabinet is incapable of bringing about good governance in the executive. Likewise, a persistent cabinet without a patient president cannot promote good governance in the executive. Thus, we greatly need persistent a president and persistent cabinet members so that together they become true torchbearers for good governance in the executive in the light of God's persistence.

As the members of the cabinet deal daily with the general public, the Lord wants them to act persistently by withholding judgement and, instead, continuing to offer forgiveness, love and grace to their fellow human beings. We all know that people have their own shortcomings, and so they need leaders who understand and deal with them patiently in line with God's will. In fact, by dealing with their people patiently, they are teaching them to behave in the same manner.

For us to see all the cabinet members shining as the real co-torchbearers for good governance in the executive, they must embrace the divine persistence as the actual benchmark of their moral behaviour, which is to guide their individual and collective actions. We badly need cabinet members who are known for their divine persistence. In order to achieve this goal, the presidency and other relevant bodies must carefully and honestly appoint people of moral integrity to man the cabinet.

But the persistence of both the chief executive and the cabinet members alone is not sufficient to bring about good governance in the executive. The bureaucracy as well should be manned by patient people. The aim of the following section is to examine the ways in which the bureaucrats can become true co-torchbearers for good governance in the executive by embracing godly patience.

Significance of the Persistence of Bureaucrats

Aware of the significant role of the bureaucracy in the executive, it would be naïve for us to speak of good governance in the executive if bureaucrats were not playing their role as worthy co-torchbearers for good governance in the light of the divine persistence. For example, when divine persistence is lacking in the personal lives of the bureaucrats, they tend to be critical and judgemental of one another, of their cabinet members and the president as well as of other members of the public. They deal impatiently with and criticize unjustly all other people. And without this significant aspect of God's love in their lives, the general masses suffer under them. They turn the nation against its own people, and in return people hate their nation. But really, what good moral values do you expect from an impatient, and hence, vindictive, team of bureaucrats? After all, the patient God is not in them and hence, not with them!

God wants all the men and women working within the bureaucracy to embrace the divine persistence as the standard of their moral values through which they are to base their daily activities. As they deal with their people on a day-to-day basis, the bureaucrats should withhold judgement and continue to offer forgiveness and reconciliation instead. That way, they will give people time to reform or improve on their moral values. By dealing persistently with the members of the public, they are really training the latter to be patient in dealing with them as well and dealing patiently with each other.

Our world seriously pines for patient bureaucrats who show their divine love as they interact with their fellow human beings. We can speak of bureaucrats as true co-torchbearers for good governance in the executive only when their moral values are saturated with the divine persistence, making it their guide in personal conduct, in their talk and even in their thought life as they relate with people daily.

At the same time, it is also imperative for all the armed forces of the executive to uphold godly patience to guide them in their conduct. They must demonstrate divine persistence in their dealings with the members of the public because good governance in the executive cannot be possible in the absence of divine persistence from them.

If we want to experience a high level of divine persistence in the lives of the bureaucrats and in the course of their work, all personnel in the armed forces, including those entrusted with recruitment to fill key positions in the nation should exemplify good ethical spirit in their work. This will help them staff these vital agencies with men and women of high moral values, especially God's persistence.

To summarize, good governance is only possible in the executive if the president, members of the cabinet and bureaucrats, among others, wholeheartedly embrace the divine persistence to guide their conduct and work. That is the only way they will be true torchbearers for good governance, emulating God's forbearance. To emphasize the importance of persistence, let's hear here from Apostle Paul: "And we urge you, brothers, warn those who are idle, encourage the timid, help the weak, be patient with everyone" (1 Thess.5:14). We are free to choose patient men and women to lead us with understanding towards our individual and collective aspirations, or we could elect impatient people to ruthlessly steer our loaded boat in a way that will make it capsize before reaching the desired seashore. The choice is ours!

Summary

Good governance is only possible and evident in and outside the executive organ of the government when the president, members of the cabinet, bureaucrats and other relevant agents such as police, military, prison and game wardens firmly embrace all the aspects of God's moral qualities—moral purity, integrity and love—as a guide to their moral values. These should be the lenses with which to evaluate national issues and tools with which to discharge their national responsibilities on a daily basis. Good people make good government, and good government brings about good governance.

But for really good governance to exist, the role of the executive branch of the government alone is not enough; the legislature and the judiciary should play their parts, too. I will therefore, devote the next section of the book (Part Two) to exploring the importance of moral qualities—purity, integrity and love—in the legislature to the realization of good governance.

PART TWO – THE LEGISLATURE
The Vitality Good Governance in the Legislature

CHAPTER 4
Moral Purity in the Legislature

CHAPTER 5
Integrity in the Legislature

CHAPTER 6
Love in the Legislature

Introduction

Legislature
It consists of all parliamentarians,
Select committees, etc.

Legislative branch, either bicameral (in the case of a legislature consisting of two chambers) or unicameral (made up of a single chamber), is responsible for enacting the laws of the state and adopting the budget for running the government. In other words, its functions also include managing the affairs of the state, such as finances (control of the public budget and expenditure), control of the executive, foreign affairs, maintaining law and order, approving treaties, etc. It is the platform for constituents, and it is led by a Speaker.

Since the legislature is composed of persons duly elected and others nominated by their people (the electorates) to represent them at national and regional assemblies, they have an inescapable obligation to make sure that the government and the nation operate well so as to enable them realize the general aspirations of their constituents and the entire state. In order to achieve these important goals and promote good governance, the parliamentarians must be provided with an enabling working environment arising from the existence of ethical practices in the legislature, the executive and the judiciary. They should be executing their national responsibilities in and through the ethical tunnel of good moral values by sacrificing their personal interests for the sake of the national vision as well as for the general welfare of the voters. In such cases, the secret behind their success is that the individual character of the parliamentarians is guided by sound ethical values. Good governance becomes the characteristic of the government.

In the event that the legislature plays its role in facilitating the smooth running of the government and the state, people enjoy security, political stability, economic prosperity, and cultural development. This situation is common in certain nations in the Western World, like the United Kingdom, Switzerland, Netherlands, USA, Canada, etc.

In some cases, members of the legislative assembly fail to deliver on their national responsibilities. This happens when they put their individual interests above national interests. They discharge their responsibilities with the wrong motive, which negatively affects the other two branches of government and their disenfranchised electorates. If this condition is not given proper and quick attention, it tears apart the legislature (loyalists versus those who are not loyal), creates animosity between the three arms of government, and makes people withdraw their allegiance on the disloyal members of the national assembly. As a result, democracy and good governance are sacrificed on the altar of selfishness. The legislative assembly becomes a symbol of poor governance in the government. At the time of my writing, this scenario is common in Africa, Asia and Middle East. In fact, political wrangles pitting the so-called "ruling party" against the "opposition" are now increasing at an alarming rate worldwide, making some states, especially in Africa, ungovernable.

In my writing, 'legislative assembly' refers to the legislative organ, while 'legislator', 'parliamentarian' or 'legislative representative' refers to the people working therein.

This part of the book deals with the way in which good governance can be realised in the legislative organ of the government by embracing the essential elements of moral purity, integrity and love. As shown in Chapter 4, good governance is possible in the legislature when all the parliamentarians wholeheartedly allow their conduct to be guided by holiness, righteousness and justice, the three principles of moral purity. That way, they will discharge well their national tasks of representation, law making, public education, supervision of the executive and constitutional and appointive functions.

If the legislators also embrace the three elements of integrity (genuineness, veracity and faithfulness) and allow them guide the execution of the duties of a parliamentarian, people will definitely experience good governance in the legislature. This will be the focus of Chapter 5.

In Chapter 6, I will explore the possibility of realizing good governance in the legislative assembly by having the legislators persistently cling to the key elements of love—benevolence, grace, mercy, persistence—to guide their individual conduct and use them as the benchmarks in the carrying out of national duties.

Chapter 4
Moral Purity in the Legislature

Compromised Legislature

Even elected leaders have not proven to be above wastage of public funds and will not hesitate to craft laws that give them unfair advantage when it comes to accessing public resources. An example of this is when they vote themselves huge salaries that gobble much of the government budget, leaving little money for development. Also when elections draw close, they join politically connected cartels and use them to plunder many sectors of the economy to fund their comeback. People who should be rooting for the underdog begin to do favours only to those who can afford to return them. Also, they refuse to accept down-to-earth solutions to economic problems if such solutions include some sacrifice on their part, like giving up some of the benefits that go with their positions. These people who are consumed with personal ambition are always doing things for their expediency, and hence, do not inspire trust in people and have made many lose faith in representative democracy.

But leaders need to die to personal ambition, not to keep

upgrading cars and wallowing in ill-gotten gains at the expense of those who elected them, hapless people who have to be overtaxed to sustain the expensive lifestyle of their leaders. Leaders need to be responsive to the needs of the electorates. Our leaders need to learn and practise godly values that will bring peace and prosperity among our people. That is the way to tip our hearts to those who fought and suffered so much for our independence. And this can only happen when legislators embrace and internalize all the essential ingredients of moral purity, integrity and love while discharging their national obligations.

Moral Purity in the Legislature

When most of the national legislators lack moral purity in their lives, the legislature can, unfortunately, be engulfed by all sorts of moral impurity. Of course, you cannot pick one or two elements of moral purity, leave the rest and by basing your ethical behaviour on it hope to become morally pure. If you want to be known for your moral purity, then build your life and personal relationships on the solid rock of holiness, righteousness and justice.

In order for us to experience moral purity in our national legislative assemblies, it is the obligation of all the electorates to vote carefully and honestly so as to choose men and women of high moral character, especially people known for holiness, righteousness and justice, to represent them. Moral purity will help them promote the spirit of good governance in and outside the legislative assembly.

I shall discuss here the processes by which good governance can be realized in the legislative assembly through embracing the three components of moral purity—holiness, righteousness and justice. Let me start with the importance of holiness in the legislature.

Holiness

Given the significance of this organ of government in the realization of the aspirations of the general public, God expects all men and women who deal with the national statutes to be holy and to carry out their national tasks as required in the Bible. In order to do so, they should consider God's holiness as the standard moral code and use it to fashion their own character and to guide the way they execute their duties.

In this book, I intend to examine good governance in the legislature in the light of God's holiness when it comes to functions, namely representation, law making, public education, supervision of the executive and constitutional and appointive functions.

Vitality of Holiness in Representation

One of the important roles of the legislature is representation, where those who are governed exercise their role in legitimising public policy through their elected members. This political representation requires the following two necessary preconditions: first, for electorates to be represented well, they must elect good representatives to represent their interests in the legislative assembly; second, the elected representatives should be good spokesmen, advising members of their constituencies concerning statutes that affect their interests, cutting the red tape of administrative procedures so that they are easily accessed by those they represent, and finding some administrative tasks and positions for them.

This, however, is not always the case. For example, when people in a constituency make a poor choice and elect an unholy person to represent them, they stifle the realization of their interests and aspirations because this depraved representative does not voice his constituents' concerns when vital national and local issues are being discussed. In other words, he does not present the views of his people before other members of parliament and does not feed them with important information that is tabled in the legislative assembly. Instead, he fritters away his tenure of office representing none other than himself, minding nothing but just his personal interests under the guise of people's representative.

Even worse, such a leader lacks good moral values to live by and impart to colleagues in the legislature. Instead, all he does is to join hands with other equally depraved legislators in prostituting their national legislature through their wicked words, deeds and even thoughts. Unfortunately, our national legislatures are currently inundated with godless people whose aim in life is to make their nations and their citizens morally impure.

For the representatives to successfully play this important role, the Lord expects them to be holy just as God is holy, for they represent His people on legislative matters. They should make God's holiness to be the standard of their character. The truth is that holy representatives are anointed leaders who preside over and represent the needs of their constituents in line with God's will. With God's backing, they help their constituents in realizing their aspirations. In addition, they are to operate as the salt and light in the legislative organ.

No nation would want political representatives who represent and protect their own selfish interests; nations are after those who genuinely represent the aspirations of their constituents. And only holy representatives in the legislature can make it possible for good governance to abound in the legislature and in the government at large.

But it is also good for good governance to exist in the law-making function of the legislature. This is the focus of the next section.

Importance of Holiness in Making the Law

One of the most important functions of the legislature is the process of making the law. This involves lengthy deliberations by members of the legislative assembly. Statutes are vital in a state's enterprise of social control. Laws may reflect private or public interests. The laws enacted may involve the general citizenry, the allocation and protection of national resources (including the wildlife), national sovereignty and international policies, etc. And so, these laws must be guided by God's commandment to man:

> So God created man in his own image, in the image of God he created him; male and female he created them. God blessed them and said to them, 'Be fruitful and increase in number; fill the earth and subdue it. Rule over the fish of the sea and the birds of the air and over every living creature that moves on the ground' (Gen. 1:27-28).

The above divine commandment has multiple teachings. For instance, it is makes it clear to the reader that God is the one who created man, and thus, He is our Creator. By creating both male and female in his image, it means that both are equal before Him, despite differences in their physical strength. Also, God has desired that human beings increase on the face of the earth. In addition, He has given man the honourable mandate of subduing the earth by ruling over the fish of the sea and the birds of the air and over every living creature that moves on the ground. It is imperative for us to note that God did not ask man to destroy animals but safeguard and control them.

However, it is unfortunate to state that man has greatly failed on this sacred responsibility by destroying and/or eliminating certain beautiful and rare creatures from the face of the earth. This deliberate disobedience to God's commands has made the Lord to curse the world. Besides the fact that they are unfavourable to non-humans, national laws that are enacted without regard to God's holiness generally lead to impurity, oppression, ungodly and dehumanising practices.

So national laws need to be seen and enacted in a better way so as to facilitate good governance. Earlier on, we saw that the legislative organ is crucial in the life of the nation. Hence, for the lawmakers to do their work for the welfare of the general populace and for them to be transparent, clean and lovable in their legislative duties, God wants them to be holy just as He is holy. This entails embracing God's holiness as the guide for their moral character. As they deliberate upon important legislative issues, some of which eventually become statutes, members of the legislature should be holy in body, soul and spirit, shunning any evil in their personal lives. But how do we get such undefiled people to become our law makers? The answer: It is by you and I keenly and sincerely looking for such people among us and, through the vote, sending them to our national assemblies.

Their holiness will enable them tackle these fundamental, legislative issues in good faith. Holiness will make legislative members put national interests and God's will above their own personal interests. If things are done in such a dignified manner by the legislators, then we can truly talk of good governance in their law-making function. But this does not negate the equally important need for holiness in the legislature's role in public education as will be seen below.

Significance of Holiness in Public Education

Another important role of the legislature is public education. Besides their constituents, legislators also represent varying interest groups. Their debates provide a platform for their constituents to air their views, be they in form of grievances, criticism or praises of government policies.

For example, since debates in parliament are covered by the media, the public gets the opportunity to know how their legislators are participating in the debate. That way, legislators, especially when probing or exploring vital policy issues or on actions of the executive, reveal to the public information the latter would have no way of accessing. Public education tends to increase the political consciousness of citizens. In some cases, it may lead to new consciousness of the duties of politics and its principal actors. This process must be done in the right way for the common benefit of the whole nation.

As legislative debates are also for the consumption of the general public, allegations or scandals must first be investigated thoroughly in camera by a given committee within the legislative assembly before getting into the public domain. The aim is to keep lies out of the legislature and to gain a desired confidence from the public. The general public need genuine political information pertaining to crucial issues that are under debate because the final results of such debates could affect them in one way or the other.

Unfortunately, most legislative assemblies have become the place where legislators proudly shame each other in the front of bewildered constituents over involvement in corrupt deals. One is named and shamed today, while the other fall into the same trap tomorrow, making a sort of vicious cycle of unedifying show. It is obvious such legislators seem to have lost the actual sense of moral purity, since they keep on assassinating each other's character in public while debating and discussing vital parliamentary issues. As such, they have nothing good to offer to themselves, much less to their own constituents and the nation in general.

What they should know is that they represent their constituencies and should defend their own images; they represent their constituents' image, and they eventually represent their nation's image in and outside their national borders. With this awareness, the legislators should seek to be effective and efficient in their work of representing the public. And to do so, they should separate themselves from all unclean things, including gossip, slur, backbiting and untrustworthiness and, instead, emulate God in holiness. They should adopt God's perfection as the standard of their moral character. That way, they will be teaching the general public to have a holy attitude towards the legislature. They will also be teaching the public to send holy representatives to the legislative assembly to deal with crucial national issues that are necessary to achieve good governance.

Good governance is only possible when the legislators debate national issues in the light of God's holiness, knowing that the Lord puts them there for the wellbeing of their nation and also for God's own glory. Our legislatures badly need God-fearing legislators to carry out their mandated role of public education. But it is better also to examine good governance in the supervision of the executive in the light of God's holiness in the following section.

Vitality of Holiness in Supervision of Executive

The other important function of the legislature is the supervision of the executive. The power of the executive has a tendency to grow, with disastrous effects. This makes it necessary for the legislature to exercise some form of control over executive power. In other words, the legislature is sanctioned legally to deal with ineffectiveness and malpractices in the executive. For instance, the legislature is supposed to exercise proper surveillance on the executive on the issue of government expenditure. Although the preparation of the national budget is initiated by the executive, the legislature, in most cases, has the near-exclusive authority of determining its final shape. A special committee of the legislature scrutinizes government spending to rein in abuses and excesses of the executive appointees. But besides financial matters, the legislature sometimes sets up special watchdog committees to oversee executive handling of certain issues of national significance.

In many instances, this noble task is not carried out by legislators who are thorough and whose character, social and business relationships are guided by God's holiness. And without this vital moral ingredient in their lives, they do their work in an impure manner. For instance, their supervision of the executive becomes an opportunity to punish those involved but not to correct their mistakes so that the systems can work well. They tend to see things upside down because they do not have a moral yardstick to help them execute their work professionally and morally. These legislators are like the unskilled medical personnel who kill their innocent patients in the name of treating them. Now, are you familiar with such legislators in your country's parliament?

For legislators to effectively play this vital responsibility on the executive, they must be of good spiritual standing and avoid being biased in any way. No one can pass moral judgement on others justly without being ethically correct himself, for the Bible says:

> Do not judge, or you too will be judged. For in the same way you judge others, you will be judged, and with the measure you use, it will be measured to you. Why do you look at the speck of sawdust in your brother's eye and pay no attention to the plank in your own eye? How can you say to your brother, 'let me take the speck out of your eye,' when all the time there is a plank in your own eye? You hypocrite, first take the plank out of your own eye, and then you will see clearly to remove the speck from your brother's eye (Matt.7: 1-5).

The above passage of Scripture shows that for the legislators to correctly execute their legislative supervisory duty on the executive, they must be holy supervisors. They must do to others what they expect them to do to them. Also, they must first set straight their ethical records so as to earn the moral right to tell the executive where it has gone wrong. That is how they will have guarded themselves from being labelled by others as hypocrites.

In reality, we are required by God to emulate His perfection, making His law the guide for our moral character. God is pure, the epitome of holiness. The whole moral code flows from His holiness. As those who are set apart by him to preside over the legislative issues of the nation, the legislators should be holy like God. Indeed, this is a biblical command that needs no negotiation but only obedience on the side of man. The Lord is overseeing the national affairs of the executive through the members of the national legislative assembly to see that things are done in the right manner.

As I end this section, it is clear to us that good governance is only possible in the government when the legislators carry out their supervisory role on the executive in the light of God's holiness. Nevertheless, for us to realise complete good governance in the legislature in the light of God's holiness, I shall now examine good governance in the constitutional and appointive functions in the light of God's holiness.

Importance of Holiness in Constitutional and Appointive Functions

There are other important legislative functions. For example, legislature can initiate additions or amendments to the national constitution or be involved in making the actual changes. Legislators amend the national constitution through laid-down procedures, which, in many cases, may involve a referendum. In addition, the legislature has the power to ratify any international treaty. Foreign agreements call for ratification, especially when they are multilateral. Any economic, political, military or environmental treaty demands legislative approval known as ratification in order to carry full legal force in a municipal law.

With regard to its appointive function, the legislature in certain countries can ratify or reject the executive appointment of key public officers, like Supreme Court judges, ambassadors, managing directors and even ministers and commissioners. Also in some cases, the legislature, through its power of impeachment, can remove the president or governor and members of the judiciary despite their being protected through the tenure of office.

These important functions of the legislature are not always carried out in the right way, especially when moral deficiencies exist in the life of members of the legislature. For example, when they lack the spirit of the divine holiness in their lives, they execute these noble tasks with little consideration of national interests. In the course of their work, they deliberately misinterpret separation of religion and government to remove God from their activities. Not knowing that in God's eyes there is no dichotomy between secular and sacred. That is how they manage to add or amend to the national constitution or participate in making some changes for their narrow interests at the very expense of national goals and the aspirations of others. Also, driven by the same unhealthy spirit, they tend to appoint, reject or impeach vital government officials without proper and acceptable grounds. Their immoral behaviour always sparks unnecessary wars between the three wings of the government.

In order to exercise these noble national obligations in the right and honourable manner, the legislators should endeavour, through the power of the Holy Spirit, to regulate their own behaviour, constraining it to be in line with God's holiness.

They should shun evil and malpractices in their own lives and in their day-to-day duties. They must take God's perfection as the standard against which to fashion their moral code.

God expects them to be holy just as He is holy. This is because God has put them in their positions to do their work for the betterment of the whole nation. To do the above functions in a God-fearing way, the legislators should portray this holiness of the Lord in their thoughts, word and conduct.

Good governance is possible when the legislators carefully execute their constitutional and appointive actions through the power derived from God's holiness. This power will enable them to achieve good governance in today's rapidly changing economic environment. In other words, in order for good governance to exist in the legislative assembly, divine holiness must pervade all the functions of the legislature. This will enable the legislators to execute their national obligations in the very light of God's holiness, for it is the only soap that can completely remove the stain of corruption from the social and political life.

In order for us to see good governance prevailing in our national legislatures in the light of holiness, it is the inescapable moral duty of all citizens to elect men and women of decent character to handle the legislative functions. Yet for us to realise proper good governance in the various functions of the legislature in the brightest light of the divine moral purity, righteousness should also have a place in the life of legislators.

Righteousness

When the national functions of the legislature are carried out in an unrighteous manner, the legislators and the entire nation will face the unpleasant consequences of their actions. One such unpleasant consequence is God's curse upon the nation. But if the legislature allows itself to be guided by the solid rock of God's righteousness, God will continually shower the nation with blessings, making it a nation whose God is the Lord (Ps.33:12). Then the citizens will enjoy peace, liberty and prosperity.

The discussion on good governance in the legislature covers representation, law-making, public education, supervision of the executive and constitutional and appointive functions. I shall discuss each in turn, starting with the representation in the light of God's righteousness.

Importance of Righteousness in Representation

"Thus you will walk in the ways of good men and keep to the paths of the righteous. For the upright will live in the land and the blameless will remain in it; but the wicked will be cut off from the land, and the unfaithful will be torn from it" (Prov. 2:20-22). The dividend of righteousness is happy life and enjoyment of one's own land and godly relationship with the righteous God. But the sure benefit of wickedness and unfaithfulness is God's wrath and curse and a doomed future.

As we all know, no one in his right mind and heart would want to be the target of God's anger and curse. So I believe representatives should choose the path of righteousness in representing constituents.

But it is unfortunate that legislators often lose the confidence that they initially enjoyed from their constituents when their actions deviate from people's expectations and for failure to conduct themselves according to what they expect of others. For instance, unrighteous legislators lack the divine righteousness in their personal lives. Their lack of righteousness is also a clear indication of the absence of God in them as well as the presence of the evil forces in their lives. So, finding themselves under the dominion of Satan, the political representatives end up failing on the important task of the representation. That is, they do not represent and meet the general aspirations of their constituents. They, instead, pursue their own interests at the expense of national goals. And as they corrupt themselves, they also corrupt their constituencies and their nation as well. Ultimately, this makes them unworthy torchbearers for good moral values and good governance in and outside the national assembly.

God requires the legislators to righteously discharge their representation duties. He wants them to diligently exercise righteousness in their representation. They are also expected to conduct themselves in conformity with what they expect of their constituents.

Since they are representing various interests of God's people, legislators should base their code of conduct on the divine righteousness so as to deal righteously with those who expressed confidence in them and gave them votes to represent them in the national assembly. If the political relationship between the legislators and the constituents is regularly maintained through divine righteousness, the process of representation can greatly benefit both parties as well as the entire nation. Unless the constituents are themselves not righteous, there is no way they would choose unrighteous people to represent them in the national assembly.

As I end this section, we should note that if the legislators act righteously, good governance in the legislative assembly is possible. Nonetheless, good governance is not complete in the legislature without examining it also in the law-making in the light of God's righteousness.

Importance of Righteousness in Law Making

As stated before, an important function of the legislature is law-making. Governments make many laws to facilitate their functions. Laws are made for the protection and welfare of people. In the economic, educational, legal, industrial, environmental fields, new laws keep on being enacted in order to deal with the ever-changing circumstances. Laws have to be amended, repealed or replaced from time to time due to domestic and external dictates.

It is the legislators who ensure there is law and order so as to make the state socially and politically stable. The importance of righteous laws is clearly depicted here by the psalmist:

> The law of the Lord is perfect, reviving the soul. The statutes of the Lord are trustworthy, making wise the simple. The precepts of the Lord are right, giving joy to the heart. The commands of the Lord are radiant, giving light to the eyes (Ps.19:7-8).

How can the legislators enact good national laws that will revitalise souls, enlighten the hearts and illuminate the eyes of the people? They can only do that by basing their moral values and legislative activities on God's righteousness.

Unrighteous legislators make unrighteous laws, and unrighteous laws create an unrighteous and ungovernable nation where citizens live in fear, and this attracts God's anger upon the land. One needs to be morally sound to be able to do what is right. What do you think of national laws which are deliberated upon and enacted by those who lack the spirit of God in their own lives? Our world is familiar with suffering today because our national legislatures are staffed by the wrong people, unrighteous men and women.

Hence, in order to successfully execute their legislative function in law-making, the Lord requires legislators to embrace divine righteousness as the standard of moral conduct. This should be the fundamental foundation on which they are to deliberate and enact national laws. Their righteousness should point to the fact that their actions are in harmony with the laws that they themselves have come up with. And they should conduct themselves according to what they expect from others by putting themselves in other peoples' shoes.

If the legislators carefully deliberate on the legislative issues in the light of God's righteousness with the aim of enacting laws in the form of statutes, good governance in the legislature and in the entire government will follow. Divine statutes are everlasting and lifesaving simply because they represent the righteousness of God who has established them. As I have stated above, unrighteous legislators make unrighteous laws, thus, attracting God's wrath upon the nation. But righteous legislators make righteous statutes for the benefit of mankind.

We seriously need legislators who do not say one thing and do another. We need legislators who are just if good governance is to thrive in the world. But good governance would be hard to realise unless the legislature was involved in the public education in the light of God's righteousness. That is the theme of the following section.

Importance of Righteousness in Public Education

Many times, majority of the legislators do not build their ethical behaviour and personal relations on God's righteousness. They tend to act and relate with others, especially their constituents, unrighteously. As they deliberate on important legislative issues, they do so with no regard to national interests and the responsibility that has been laid upon them. This makes the general public despise and shun any news coming from the national legislative assembly, assuming it lacks moral credibility.

As established in our discussion concerning the need for public education, it is important to understand that for legislators to carry out their noble obligation in an honourable and sacred manner, they should embrace God's righteousness as their standard of moral character. This means that their personal actions should be in agreement with the laws they have enacted. And they must conduct themselves in conformity with what they expect of others. In addition, it is imperative for them to approach all their legislative debates in the light of God's righteousness. As they do their work, they are to know very well that they are actually educating the public about socio-economic and political issues. They should not mislead the general masses through deceptive gimmicks while debating serious national matters. Instead, their words and conduct should reflect righteousness.

The legislators can only win the hearts and souls of the public if they righteously approach their debates on crucial political issues in the legislature. By doing so, they are actually fulfilling their vital legislative role of educating the public socially and politically. This process will, in turn, teach the public to adopt God's righteousness as their unique code of moral character and behave righteously when dealing with national issues.

When the legislators execute public education in this dignified and righteous manner, we have reason to speak of the presence of good governance in the legislature in particular and in the government in general. Our legislatures desperately need righteous legislators to perform this noble legislative role of public education.

But we cannot comfortably speak of good governance in the legislature when it does not exist in the legislative function of the legislature's supervision of the executive. That is the theme of the following section.

Importance of Righteousness in Supervision of Executive

As we know very well, the legislators are supposed to exercise diligent surveillance over the executive in issues pertaining to finance and other matters. But this is only possible if the one who is supposed do the supervision is more qualified than the one being supervised; he should have better indicators upon which he bases his supervision. For instance, God qualifies to supervise the affairs of man because, besides being the Creator of the universe, He is omniscient and righteous. Therefore, the first logical question for anyone to ask is, "What merits the legislators to supervise the executive?"

Unfortunately, most members of the legislature lack the Spirit of God in their personal lives. As a result, their moral values naturally get inclined towards the acts of the sinful nature. They do not exercise any restraint when they feel nudged to do what is wrong in their daily activities. This makes their working environment and legislative matters always subject to criticism by the honest onlookers. For instance, whenever an external audit is carried out in the legislature in many parts of the world, findings are generally alarming, revealing massive corruption. This is not to mention sexual immorality, theft, slander, deception and acts of selfishness.

These are the obvious consequences of the unrighteousness of the legislators. To rephrase the above question, "Do you believe that such unrighteous legislators have moral right to honestly and logically supervise the activities of the executive organ?"

To answer the above question satisfactorily, the legislators should possess the divine righteousness of God as an aspect of their moral purity. Then this should be the lenses through which to view the activities of the executive organ. The righteousness of the legislators should show that their actions are in line with the state laws that they have enacted. Most often, the so-called "watchdogs" are completely "blind dogs." Thus, instead of watching externally, they look inwardly and so give their biased and myopic reports on significant national matters. For them to see clearly and squarely, they must have divine righteousness, inner and external eyes to appraise public matters righteously for the welfare of the entire nation and for the glory of God.

Good governance in the supervision of the executive is only possible when the legislators exercise their surveillance over the executive activities through the light of God's righteousness. Our legislatures seriously need righteous men and women to supervise the daily activities of the executive organs so as to stamp out evil that emanates from chronic corruption of human beings. But in order to ensure complete good governance in the legislature, we need it also in the constitutional and appointive functions.

Importance of Righteousness in the Constitutional and Appointive Functions

When most of the legislators lack God's righteousness in their lives, their social and business relationships, accordingly, are characterized by corruption. They also lack the righteous Lord in their lives. This makes them weak morally, surrendering themselves to all the promptings of evil forces. Their words and actions are said and done in very unrighteous manner. For example, they execute important legislative functions of the constitutional and appointive not for the general good of the nation but to satisfy their individual egos. Of course, you don't expect an unrighteous person to do things rightly. So their unrighteousness makes the entire legislature equally unrighteous in the eyes of God and also in the eyes of the general public. And when the legislature is unrighteous, then the whole government is likely to become unrighteous, too.

Thus, in order to do the above important national and constitutional duties in a righteous way, the legislators must be immersed in the righteousness of God. That is, they must be righteous like God because they are given their roles by the Almighty God so as to manage His people in the right way for the national benefit. Truly, righteous people have no evil plans whose aim is to fail or harm others, for they love others as themselves and love to do right always.

God truly wants the legislators to operate in a conducive and transparent atmosphere of dignified righteousness as they execute their constitutional and appointive functions. Good governance in the constitutional and appointive functions is enhanced by the legislators initiating additions and amendments to existing laws when necessary and ensuring that such changes are guided by the desire for righteousness.

Nations need not only rhetoric legislators but sincere and righteous legislators, people who participate in legislative activities that are in line with God's righteousness. Only then can we correctly speak of good governance in and outside the legislative assemblies.

Good governance is, therefore, only possible in the legislature when the functions of the legislature—representation, law-making, public education, supervision of the executive and constitutional and appointive functions—are fully executed in accordance with God's righteousness. Without righteous legislators to execute these vital tasks, our legislative system will be a mockery.

But for us to realise truly good governance within and beyond the four corners of the legislative branch of the government, it is important that the legislature be saturated with divine justice, the last ingredient of moral purity.

Justice

As I mentioned before, legislature is one of the most important of the three branches of the government.

It is mandated to carry out a host of functions, including: representation, law-making, public education, supervision of the executive, and constitutional and appointive functions. If these vital functions are carried out by the legislators without consideration for God's justice, destruction of people will ensue because peaceful coexistence and justice go together.

But if these legislative functions are planned and executed according to God's justice, people's interests and aspirations will be fulfilled, and the whole nation will flourish in love, justice, equality and equity and economic and political prosperity.

Let us now explore the importance of God's justice in representation and its role in bringing about good governance in the legislature.

Importance of Justice in Representation

Although constituents trust and depend on their political representatives, legislators sometimes dishonour and discount the confidence and trust bestowed upon them by their constituents by failing to deliver what they had promised to do when soliciting for votes. Instead, they put their personal interests in the fore. And when the people who are supposed to uphold and enforce divine justice among the people become involved in injustice, justice in the nation becomes mere rhetoric.

When this crucial legislative function of the people's representation is not carried out in line with justice by the legislators, the pertinent constituents' interests and aspirations are jeopardised. This is simply because their unjust representatives find themselves without the desire to speak for and represent people in a just way in the national legislative forum. They instead fail on this dignified legislative obligation by putting their own personal goals above the goals of their constituencies as well as above the national vision. When this occurs, they unfortunately let down their constituents and the entire nation. We don't expect just representation of any kind to come through the words and the deeds of unjust person, do we?

We should back our words with actions, showing that we are serious with what we say with the words of our mouth. The world badly yearns for legislators who practise divine justice as they represent their constituents in the legislative assemblies.

In order for the legislative representatives to fulfil their roles successfully and maintain the confidence of their respective constituents, they must take God's justice as the standard of their moral character. Also, they must take divine justice as their official emblem before they ask their subjects to adhere to the same standard. Once more, they must fairly administer justice among people as they carry out their day-to-day national activities. They should clearly know that as they allow themselves to be guided by God's justice as they play their representation role, they are actually teaching the general populace to take the divine justice seriously, making it the cornerstone of their own moral character.

Good governance is only possible in the legislative representation when the legislators seriously emulate God's justice by internalising the essence of justice into their own lives and representing their constituents in the light of God's justice. We do not want witty legislative representatives but rather those who truly cherish and practise godly justice. An unjust person has no moral authority to represent others, especially on just matters and important national issues. But to realise truly good governance in the legislature, justice should exist in the law-making function of the legislature as well.

Importance of Justice in Law-Making

The worst laws that I have ever seen are the ones selfishly and hurriedly made to protect the selfish interests of the lawmakers themselves. Such laws end up being harmful to the very people whom the lawmakers were supposed to represent. In other words, in most cases the legislators do not make inclusive laws for the betterment of the whole nation because they do not exercise this noble function in the light of God's justice. Such are oppressive and tyrannical laws which are always short-lived and predestined to fail.

To underscore the importance of exercising care so as to make just and righteous laws, it took God's servant Moses 40 days and 40 nights of no eating and drinking on the mountain for God to give him the flawless Ten Commandments that are the ultimate guide for love (Exod. 34:28). Of course God did not need time and effort to produce these divine laws, but Moses as a human being needed to humble himself before God to qualify receiving them.

Just laws, like God's statutes, are made by just people in the light of God's justice to protect the general and specific aspirations and needs of the entire citizenry and other creatures and special interest groups. Laws should be crafted in such a way that they not only protect national interests but also international interests. Just laws protect and bind all the people, including leaders; no one should be above the law. The laws should be perfect, trustworthy and right as to make the general public delight in them. When just legislators enact laws in a loving manner, guided by justice, they thus, ease the work of the judiciary when it comes to interpreting and applying them. But unjust laws are hard to implement without causing friction between the lawmakers, the judiciary and the executive.

Furthermore, enduring laws need patience, meticulousness and a loving spirit on the part of legislators during their lengthy formulation and enacting process. Moreover, lawmakers are to make them with the future in mind. They must know that national laws are very expensive and not easy to amend or rescind.

In their lengthy deliberations with the eventual aim of enacting laws in the form of statutes, the legislators are expected to do their work in the light of God's justice. Like God, they are to uphold and wear the crown of the divine justice before they expect others to adopt it as the cornerstone of their ethical behaviour. This is simply because if they are unable to practice the divine justice in their own lives, they cannot create just national laws that represent and protect the interests of the various sections of the population.

Our world badly requires legislatures that cherish godly justice in and outside the legislative assemblies. We need legislatures that honestly practise what they preach, honouring all their words and promises as they represent their people on pertinent legislative issues.

Good governance becomes evident in the law-making process when the legislators deliberate and enact laws in the light of God's justice for the benefit of the entire nation and also for God's glory. Again, our world thirsts for just legislatures to make just statutes. We surely cannot talk of good governance in the law-making function of the legislature if the legislators are deliberately unjust in their individual behaviour as well as in their legislative practices. Let just men and just women make just national laws for the betterment of mankind!

Nevertheless, apart from obtaining good governance in the law-making process guided by God's justice, it is also important that there be justice in the legislature's role of public education.

Importance of Justice in Public Education

In this technological world, when an important policy issue is under debate in a legislative assembly, citizens attentively watch it on their TV sets, listen from their radio sets and read about it in the print media. The deliberations are given sufficient coverage so as to fully make people understand what is happening in their nation. But with regard to this crucial legislative function, dishonest legislators may sometimes use their debates to misinform the public, badly failing on their important role of the public education.

But on the other hand, honest legislators deliberate on the legislative matters guided by God's justice and let the general public know what they are doing. If the citizens discover that the legislators are dishonest in the way they debate policy issues and educate the general public, they will automatically lose confidence in them. But if the legislators wear the crown of God's justice in their own lives as they approach legislative matters, they will impart the same divine justice to the affairs of the public and win people's confidence in return.

It is very unfortunate to note here that often legislators lack the divine justice in their personal lives. This makes them impure, as God's justice is an important part of moral purity. Also, it makes them lack the Spirit's anointing over their lives as well as in their national tasks.

Thus, as they carry out this vital legislative mission of discussing and deliberating over national parliamentary affairs in the eyes of the watchful public, the legislators treat and relate to each other unjustly. The issues they discuss lack God's justice in them, and the general public is not fed with the actual truth but mere lies and rumours. In other words, the legislature becomes unjust to itself and to the entire nation, making the citizens lose faith in the legislative function of public education. But what moral justice do you expect unjust legislators to impart to their citizens, their whole nation and other human beings? To address this moral issue, it is the sole duty of the electorates to choose men and women of good moral standing to man their legislatures and educate them on crucial national matters.

Before they require others to take God's justice as the yardstick for their moral conduct, the legislators must uphold the divine justice as they carry out their legislative activities. Their lives should reflect the true nature of the way they deliberate on policy issues. The Lord expects the legislators to execute their debates in the legislative assembly, no matter how long they are, under the guidance of divine justice. This is to enable them pass on to the general public the essence of godly justice and good governance together with the political messages through the legislative function of the public education.

By way of summarizing the foregoing, it is important to know that good governance is only achievable in the public education function when legislators base their personal code of conduct on divine justice, for this will help them to carry out their legislative debates justly. We seriously need righteous legislatures to implement their dignified function of public education in accordance with the divine justice. Yet we cannot truly talk of good governance in the legislature if legislators are not properly carrying out their role of supervising the executive, guided by God's justice.

Importance of Justice in the Supervision of Executive

Another important role of the legislature is the supervision of the executive. In this case, a high level of justice is necessary. The main goal of the supervision is to see the executive affairs through just and honest independent eyes so as to identify any problems early enough and help the executive organ address them before they evolve into a crisis. The primary purpose of supervision is not to deal with those who cause problems in a ruthless and unjust manner but to put in place measures to hinder wrongdoing.

The legislature, however, is not always guided by justice as it carries out this noble task on the executive affairs. Instead, it heavily relies on suspicion, hatred, selfishness, envy and bias, among others. For instance, most of the time the legislature supervises the affairs of the executive organ not primarily to point out any shortcomings and suggest solutions but so as to punish and shame those concerned. This unhealthy and unjust attitude of the legislature oftentimes makes the executive revenge severely on the legislators. It also makes the executive hide its operations from the legislature to avoid unjust grilling.

If the relationship between the key branches of government is not based on fairness and justice, it is hard for any nation to attain the necessary smooth coordination of the three organs (executive, legislature and judiciary) of the state. These organs need checks and balances to ensure that none abuses its roles and becomes unduly stronger than others. The separation of powers is achieved in the differences in the personnel, control and functions. But when the necessary coordination between the three important branches of the government is lacking, the government operates in an uncoordinated way, which could lead to its collapse. As we can see here, the three pillars of government badly need to coordinate their strengths and weaknesses together and ensure harmony among themselves for the common good of the government.

Therefore, for the legislators to carry out an unbiased supervision of the executive, they must first adopt God's justice as their guide in and outside the legislative assembly. This is because it is not possible to justly supervise the activities of the executive if those who are doing the supervising are themselves not guided by divine justice. Indeed, one cannot teach what they do not know. In other words, the legislature must truly saturate itself and all its activities and carry out this vital role of the supervision of the executive in the very light of God's justice before requiring the executive to adhere to the same moral standard of work.

In summary, for good governance to thrive in the supervision of the executive, the legislators must espouse divine justice as the fundamental rule of their work of supervising the executive. To be worthy watchdogs, our legislatures should be guided by God's justice. And for this to happen, we should always send to the legislative assembly people with recognisable moral justice.

But before I am done with the discussion of good governance in the legislature, let us explore the importance of the legislative role of constitutional and appointive function in the next section.

The Importance of Justice in Constitutional and Appointive Functions

In most instances, legislators carry out these important functions with the underlying motive of benefiting themselves as individuals instead of seeking to realize national aspirations. For example, legislators are often biased in their appointive role, unjustly approving or refusing to approve the appointment of important government officials who favour or disfavour the interests of such legislators. Other times, they initiate discussions that lead to certain amendments to the national constitution or vigorously fight for changes, not for the common good of the nation and her citizens but simply to attain their selfish interests.

Naturally, conflict ensues in such unfriendly political environment and causes unnecessary tension or even loss of lives among the citizens. In some cases, this unhealthy political situation may eventually lead to unhealthy groupings within the population and ultimately to the collapse of government. This is because the legislators do not base their work on justice but on ulterior motives.

Therefore, as these important functions directly affect both the executive and the judiciary in one way or the other, and because of the importance of stability in the government as well as in the entire nation, the legislature should always seek to be led by justice as it discharges its roles. It should make justice roll on like a river and righteousness like a mighty stream (Amos 5:24) for the common good of the entire nation as well as for God's own glory.

In order to play these significant functions justly, the legislators must base their individual lives and the legislative activities on the divine justice before they expect others to do the same. In other words, they are to embrace God's justice as the trademark of their own actions before they expect the general public to emulate the same divine justice. Likewise, they are to treat others fairly as they carry out their legislative functions because this is what God wants. They should be fair and just in the administration of the constitutional and appointive functions by showing no partiality. By acting justly as good role model for the divine justice, the legislators will make the others see sense in embracing this important spiritual code of conduct.

Good governance is possible in the constitutional and appointive functions only when the legislators base their actions on God's justice and initiate additions and amendments to the law and actively participate in approving or rejecting the appointment of key government officials. Our legislatures thirst for men and women who act justly as they tackle legislative issues for the betterment of human beings.

To conclude this discussion, when the functions of the legislature are guided by all the aspects of moral purity—holiness, righteousness and justice—good governance exists in this organ of government. It is therefore, our primary task to always staff our national assemblies with people of moral purity, people who are intent on addressing national issues selflessly and with fairness.

But we cannot realise the actual presence of good governance unless the same legislative functions are fully submerged in the oasis of the divine integrity and love. In the next section, I intend to look into the ways in which the three elements of integrity can influence good governance in the representation, law-making, public education, supervision of the executive, constitutional and appointive functions of the legislature.

Chapter 5
Integrity in the Legislature

As for you, if you walk before me in integrity of heart and uprightness, as David your father did, and do all I command and observe my decrees and laws, I will establish your royal throne over Israel for ever... (1 Ki. 9:4-5).

For the continuity of their rule and power in their specific countries and for the welfare of God's people as well as for the glory of God, legislators need to walk in integrity of heart and uprightness before God and man. Failure to this, the legislature and the entire nation will fall into the deepest pit of moral corruption.

But in order for us to realise good governance in our various national parliaments, it is the inescapable duty of all national electorates to vote wisely and responsibly so as to put in key positions men and women who adhere to ethical norms—for instance, genuineness, veracity and faithfulness. Wrong electoral choices corrupt the legislative systems, in particular, and the entire government systems in general.

In this chapter, I intend to examine the importance of the presence of divine integrity in the legislature in the pursuit of good governance in and outside the legislative system. This will involve exploring in detail the possibility of having good governance in each function of the legislature that is characterized by genuineness, veracity and faithfulness.

Genuineness

In case the national legislature does not completely base its activities on God's genuineness, all its functions will lack the essence of realness in them. And this is just what is expected of an unrealistic legislative body. Conversely, a realistic national assembly bases its functions on the spirit of the divine genuineness, leading to national unity, equality and prosperity as the nation enjoys unlimited blessings from God.

In the clear light of the divine genuineness, I shall examine the essence of good governance in the representation, law-making, public education, supervision of the executive, constitutional and appointive roles of the legislature. In the next section, let me look at good governance in the legislative representation in the light of God's genuineness, the first element of integrity.

Importance of Genuineness in Representation

In our world, do we have real and authentic representatives who can genuinely represent the views, needs and aspirations of their constituents in the legislative forums? As important function of the legislature, genuine representation refers to the process in which every citizen is equally and authentically represented in the legislative assembly, thus, safeguarding the interests of everybody.

But the legislators frequently abuse this important legislative function and instead of seeking to address the collective needs and aspirations of their constituents they use their offices to pursue their own selfish interests. For example, the lack of the divine genuineness in the lives of the legislators indicates the absence of God's integrity in them. Without this vital moral ingredient in their personal behaviours, the legislators have no acceptable moral values to help them represent their constituents in the right way. Their words and deeds cannot be trusted. And when the constituents are let down by their legislative representatives, they lose confidence and hope in them and decide not to elect them again.

To avoid this sad state of affairs, God demands that legislative members be genuine to themselves, to Himself and to their people. They are expected to be what they are in everything, including their own words, deeds and thoughts. In this case, they are to honestly deliver to their voters what they have previously promised to them in election campaigns. On the whole, they must adopt God's genuineness as the basic foundation upon which they are to build their moral character. And this divine genuineness should be the fundamental apparatus with which they are to carry out their legislative representation.

Good governance is only possible in the legislative representation when men and women who are working in the legislative branch of the government adopt God's genuineness as their personal ethical code of conduct as they represent the aspirations of their constituents in the legislative assembly. In our legislative assemblies, we need men and women whose integrity reflects their genuineness. However, we should not only wish them to be there but should use our votes to take them there. During the election, we should seek to elect genuine men and women and send them to promote the spirit of genuineness in our national legislative assemblies. Credible legislators create credible legislatures!

In the next section, let us see the role of genuineness in the law-making process.

Importance of Genuineness in Law Making

Legitimate national laws are a reflection of the laws of God. But can such laws be made by people who are full of moral flaws? No! Jesus Christ says:

> Watch out for false prophets. They come to you in sheep's clothing, but inwardly they are ferocious wolves. By their fruit you will recognize them. Do people pick grapes from thorn bushes, or figs from thistles? Likewise every good tree bears good fruit, but a bad tree bears bad fruit. A good tree cannot bear bad fruit, and a bad tree cannot bear good tree (Matt. 7:15-18).

Very often when legislators are formulating and enacting laws, they do not put into consideration the genuine aspirations of their constituents so as to provide proper provisions within the state laws that protect individual and public interests. Instead, they make laws that only safeguard their narrow, private interests, which means they put their aspirations above the national interests.

Yet what such egocentric legislators ought to understand is that unfair laws always lead to discontent in the nation and disproportionate development within the geographical boundaries of the same country. This makes people lose confidence and trust in the men and women who constitute their own legislature. This could also bring about unhealthy consequences upon the nation as a result of God's wrath.

God expects the legislative function of the government to be genuine, as it deals with deliberations and the crafting of statutes. In other words, the Lord requires the legislators to adopt godly genuineness as part of their moral character so that they can be true to themselves before God and man. This is simply because the state laws they make are the ones to guide in the solution of social and political problems and to create some important landmarks in the enterprise of social control. In fact, "Leadership ultimately rests on trust. People choose to follow leaders they trust."[12]

We should understand that for a complete good governance to exist in the law-making branch of the legislature, the legislators must honestly adopt Biblical genuineness as the true mark of their ethical code of conduct through which they are to carry out their law-making exercise in the legislative assembly. The world greatly thirsts for such true legislators who can deliberately enact genuine laws as the state statutes. This calls for all voters to ensure that they sponsor and vote for morally dignified people to man our legislatures for the benefit of mankind.

Nonetheless, we cannot speak of complete good governance in the legislature if it does not exist in the public education, guided by godly genuineness.

The Importance of Genuineness in Public Education

Public education is another major function of the legislature. However, debates are often characterized by lies and biases resulting from conflicts among legislators. And when truth becomes a casualty in public debates, we are justified to say that the legislature's crucial role of public education is not being carried out with genuineness. Instead of giving the correct socio-economic and political position in the country, legislators give the citizens a deceptive picture. Regrettably, when the public discovers it is not being given the correct information, it loses faith in the legislature.

For instance, in the early years of the Sudan People's Liberation Army and Sudan People's Liberation Movement (SPLA/M),

---

12 Ibid.,Blackaby, 84.

revolutionary and political messages were spiced with some lies so as to entice the general masses to join the movement, and in fact, a lot of people did join it. But since lies have a short lifespan, it took just a short period of time for the masses to establish the truth. However, the funny thing is that though the deceived Sudanese succeeded in knowing the truth, they totally failed to distinguish between the lies and the actual meaning of politics. To this day, whenever you share a sort of doubted idea with people in South Sudan, especially rural civilians, they are ever suspicious and their reply is always, "You are using us to do politicking," meaning, "You are telling us lies." What they need to know, however, is that politics cannot be equated with lies, for it means, among others, the practice or study of the art and science of forming, directing and administering states and other political units; the art and science of government; political science.

But since the political commissars abused this noble legislative function of public education, the people of South Sudan have lost faith in it, and it will take a long time to change their current distorted attitude towards the word 'politics'. It takes a long time to build the image of integrity, but it takes an equally long time to regain it when it is lost.

Given the above example from the history of the SPLA/M as well as the actual meaning of public education, it is imperative that legislators base their activities on godly genuineness as they discharge their important function of public education. Legislators should always maintain their true image as they deal with the legislative matters and interact with other people. They must clearly understand that God's genuineness is one of the basic elements of divine integrity, and God expects them to live it out.

True good governance is only possible in the public education of the legislature when legislators adopt God's genuineness as the fundamental cornerstone of their personal lives as well as the best light by which to tackle their national and legislative issues. Our legislatures desperately need people who wholeheartedly uphold God's genuineness as the basis of their moral values. In other words, they must be true to themselves, true to God, and true to others in their day-to-day activities. Let's not send unreal people to our parliaments and expect the institutions to make them real!

But in order to realize completely good governance in the legislature, it should carry out its role of supervision of the executive in the light of God's genuineness.

Importance of Genuineness in the Supervision of Executive

As a key organ of any political system, the legislature should honestly exercise its supervisory role over the activities of the executive in the light of God's genuineness. But due to personal differences and corruption, the legislature sometimes plays its role of supervision of the executive in a biased way by either allowing the executive to misuse vital national resources or by failing to provide reliable watchdog committee to exercise surveillance over some significant areas of the executive. Also, based on individual interests of the legislators, the legislature often knowingly permits the president to sign some unbeneficial international treaties on behalf of the state. On the other hand, it can deny the executive from doing things that are beneficial to the nation. These few examples are some of the dread consequences when legislators generally lack godly genuineness in their own lives.

How do we expect them to show some signs of moral integrity and responsible actions in their legislative tasks if they are not daily driven by the essence of moral genuineness? The civil servants working in the legislature cannot, of course, faithfully execute their supervisory role on the affairs of the executive if they lack divine genuineness. For them to carry out their work in line with God's will and for the betterment of mankind, they must cherish God's genuineness as the significant basis of their own lives. It must also be the only light through which they implement their supervision of the executive. This is simply because for one to supervise others' activities in a given field of life, that person must possess some valuable expertise which qualifies him to exercise his unbiased supervision in that particular area. Therefore, it is very imperative for the legislators to wear the actual gown of God's genuineness before they act as dignified watchdogs over the affairs of the executive.

Proper supervision of the executive becomes possible when the legislative members take God's genuineness as the fundamental basis of their own personal character. That time, the legislative and national issues are seen in light of God's genuineness. Genuine supervision of the executive is what the Lord requires because it brings glory to His name and prosperity to the nation. If we really want this significant legislative role to be done genuinely, then we must make sure that we always staff our legislatures with genuine men and women so as to reap what we sow! The same should happen in respect of the constitutional and appointive functions of the legislature.

Importance of Genuineness in Constitutional and Appointive Functions

The right question to ask here is whether the legislatures always demonstrate the necessary integrity to fairly carry out constitutional and appointive functions. In some cases, the legislature fails on this crucial function, either by initiating biased additions or amendments to the constitution or refusing to participate at the level that they should in making such changes because of their hidden personal interests. Also, due to their hidden selfish aspirations, the legislators often selfishly block the appointment or removal of some key government officials.

When the legislature fails to honour their responsibilities, unnecessary ill tension appears between the executive and the legislature as well as among some citizens. In the event of such political and social friction within the government and among people, chances are that the government may collapse because God and innocent people cannot be happy with this unhealthy condition. Those are some of the symptoms of bad governance.

In order to avoid such bad governance in the government, the legislature must take God's genuineness as the foundation on which both constitutional and appointive functions are determined. In other words, for the legislature to base itself on the divine genuineness, all its men and women should adopt such genuineness as their moral code of conduct as they operate before God and man – they must be true in whatever they say, in whatever they do and in the way they think. Doing this will bring God's blessings upon the nation.

Good governance in the constitutional and appointive functions of the legislature is only possible if all men and women working in the legislature uphold the divine genuineness as the standard of their ethical values. It is also possible in the legislature when all legislative issues are conducted transparently and accountably. Legislators should not deliberately ignore God's genuineness and still expect to have moral integrity.

In summary, we should know that good governance is realized only when the representation, law-making, public education, supervision of the executive and constitutional and appointive functions of the legislature are guided by God's genuineness. In order for these important legislative roles to be discharged properly, let's us always send genuine people to our national legislatures.

In the next section, let us see the importance of the role of veracity, the element of the divine integrity in the good governance of the legislature.

Veracity

Veracity, the second element of divine integrity, is one of the precious ingredients of moral values needed among the sons and the daughters of men, and it often misses in the legislatures of our national governments. God requires His people to be honest under all circumstances as they relate to Him, as they interact with each other and as they carry out their national and personal obligations.

Here I seek to prove how the firm application of veracity in all the functions of the legislature can usher in the spirit of good governance in and outside the premises of the legislative system. In doing so, let me first examine the quintessence of good governance in the representation in the light of veracity.

Importance of Veracity in Representation

The legislators are elected by their constituents to represent their respective narrow and wide interests in the national assembly. Honesty is the fundamental fabric that firmly ties together the electorates and their representatives in the implementation of this vital role of the legislative representation.

But the legislators sometimes let their constituents down by failing to fulfil their legislative obligations, not representing people's interests before the legislature. Instead, the legislators represent their own selfish aspirations before none other than themselves. This is caused by the lack of the divine justice in the life of the legislature as well as through the crooked ways in which some legislators are wrongly nominated and elected during marred and dishonest processes of national elections.

Wherever there is no veracity, there is mismanagement, corruption and mistrust between the legislators and the constituents, bringing the nation down to her knees.

Our global legislatures need men and women who from the bottom of their hearts uphold godly veracity as the cornerstone of their moral character and who act as the admirable role model for their own national citizens. Such trustworthy legislators must fulfil their national duties or social responsibilities by honestly representing the interests of their constituents. By doing this, they put national interest above their own personal aspirations. They must present things just the way they really are, whether they are talking about themselves or other things concerning their nation. They must be constantly honest under all circumstances as they deal with themselves, as they commune with their God, as they interact with the members of their constituencies and as they perform their legislative issues. Honesty is one of the fundamental foundations upon which genuine legislative representation is established.

Only when all the narrow interests of the private sector or the general public are fully represented in the parliament, when the wider interests of the common sectors of the entire public are honestly represented within the four corners of the legislature and only when national interests are put above individual interests in the legislature can we speak of good governance in the representation in the light of God's veracity. Above all, only when the Almighty God is pleased with the manner in which the legislators execute their representative roles among His people can we justifiably talk of good governance in the representation that is guided by God's veracity. Let's therefore, staff our legislatures with honest men and women for good governance to abound in our nations! Let us now explore the role of veracity in law-making.

Importance of Veracity in Law Making

In most cases, our national laws are deliberated and enacted as national statutes by men and women who lack God's veracity in their personal character. Lack of this vital moral element in their lives means that their social and business relationships are built on moral dishonesty. This makes them dishonest with themselves, dishonest with their own constituents, dishonest with their own nation, dishonest with the national laws they make and even dishonest with their own Creator. The laws that are made by dishonest legislators naturally lack the spirit of the divine veracity, which is an important aspect of godly integrity. As a result, these immoral laws are oppressive to the members of the general public, especially the weak and the poor. They promote all sorts of moral corruption and act as a snare for the nation.

Divine veracity or honesty is one of the solid cornerstones upon which the law-making function of the legislature should be established and firmly based. The truth of the matter is that the legislature cannot justly discuss and enact useful statutes to facilitate social cohesion and political control and also address social and national problems adequately if they are not guided by God's veracity. Thus, for the national laws to represent the will of the Lord, the legislators must completely cherish the divine veracity and adopt it as the permanent basis for their ethical character and reliable vessel through which they are to carry out their law-making activities.

When the legislature carries out its law-making function in the light of God's veracity, the national law shows its true colour as being below none other than the Lord himself. Then it plays its real role as the respecter of no man, including the executive president, making all people to have equal attention before it.

It is fair for us to comprehend that just legislature produces just laws for the general welfare of the human beings and also for God's own glory. If the legislators fail to put and weigh the state statutes on an honest scale during the actual formulation and enacting of the national laws in the national legislature, all the relevant law enforcing agencies will proportionately interpret and apply them unjustly, for the height and shape of a building is normally determined by its foundation.

As I draw towards the end of this discussion, we are to know that good governance in the law-making is only possible in the legislature if God's veracity becomes a firm basis on which national laws are discussed and passed as statutes governing the solution of social and political problems and ensuring some social control. It is also possible when all the legislators cherish divine honesty and take it as the cornerstone of their own ethical code of conduct. If we want to be governed and protected by just national laws, we must choose loyal citizens among ourselves to represent us in our national assemblies.

Nevertheless, good governance in the legislature would be incomplete without godly veracity in public education. That is the focus of the next section.

Importance of Veracity in Public Education

If the members of the legislative assembly are not guided by divine veracity in carrying out legislative matters like public education, the general masses remained uninformed, since they will not be privy to important debates in parliament. For example, when a motion is tabled in parliament by a member who is known for being dishonest, colleagues in the same house, first of all, will not take him and his motion seriously for lack of faith in him. Members of the public will also view him and his motion in the same way. Even if the motion of this member could benefit people, his reputation of dishonesty will hinder its passage. It is even worse if the honesty of the entire legislature were to be questionable in the eyes of the general public: the vital role of public education is greatly jeopardised.

Seriously, it is not possible for dishonest members of the legislative assembly to honestly educate the general public on parliamentary affairs. And when people are fed with wrong public education, they begin to dismiss all legislative debates as lies. Worse still, feeding the public with falsehood makes them to innocently take the wrong side on national and political issues. And once they discover that the legislators knowingly mislead them on crucial legislative matters, they lose faith in the legislature. In other words, the citizenry eventually lose trust in members of parliament and the legislative system as a whole.

For the legislature to execute meaningful public education among members of the public, it is, therefore, paramount for the legislators to embrace God's veracity to always guide their conscience and behaviour as individuals. In order to carry out decent public education before man and God, the legislators should keep their tongues from evil and their lips from speaking lies (Ps. 34:13).

Legislators ought to be known by their constituents for being honest as they interact with the people they represent, as they deal with each other in the legislative assembly and as they carry out their legislative duties and as they commune in faith with their God, the honest Creator. As they seek to educate the general public about some important parliamentary issues, God expects them to present things as they really are, whether they are speaking of themselves or of their work. They must portray their real self in all situations, and their honesty will subsequently radiate through the whole legislative system, making it conducive for fair public education.

In summary, good governance in the legislature demands that the legislature properly carry out its role of public education in light of God's veracity. Men and women in the legislative assembly should embrace divine veracity as the foundation upon which to base their ethical values. Good governance is attainable when the whole legislative body takes God's veracity as the cornerstone of its legislative work and for guiding debates in parliament. In short, good governance is possible in the legislature when public education is guided by godly veracity. Dishonest people are the best promoters of falsehoods; hence, we cannot afford to entrust them with the responsibility of disseminating important information regarding national matters.

Nonetheless, in order to achieve proper good governance in the legislature, it is good for us to also ensure that supervision of the executive is carried out in the light of God's veracity.

Importance of Veracity in Supervision of Executive

The fourth function of the legislature is the supervision of the executive. The way the social and political affairs of the executive branch of the government are carried out need close monitoring.

Unfortunately, members of the legislative assembly are occasionally biased in their supervision of the executive due to lack of honesty on their part. Certainly, a dishonest person cannot have unbiased surveillance over the affairs of another person simply because he will have been disqualified by lack of sound moral values. Because of the absence of divine veracity in his personality, he cannot clearly and honestly distinguish between what is morally good and what is morally corrupt. And we correctly judge dishonesty by looking at it through the magnifying glass of God's veracity.

With that awareness, let's go deeper in exploring the problem. When dishonest legislators supervise the affairs of the executive branch of the government, they cause more harm than good to the nation. Since they have no good moral eyes and ears to help them do the right job, they mess up the work and thus, infuriate the members of the executive. Subsequently, the executive declines to cooperate with the dishonest legislature by doing everything possible to frustrate the supervision exercise. But what will happen when there is disunity of mind and heart between them? Of course, the normal result is that the government will not do its work harmoniously.

The Lord requires the legislators to be completely honest in their personal lives so as to present things as they really are. That is, he wants their divine veracity to be self-evident in that whatever they say can pass the test—they should be honest in every circumstance. In addition, they should be truthful in what they formally proclaim as well as in what they suggest.

The fact of the matter is that any social or political system is composed of people—of course, no system is a system in the absence of people. Accordingly, it is the legislators who make up the legislature. Thus, their veracity can transform the legislature to be honest in all its operations. People serve God by serving His people through dealing with them honestly and truthfully, as St. Paul says in his letter:

> Rather, we have renounced secret and shameful ways; we do not use deception, nor do we distort the word of God. On the contrary, by setting forth the truth plainly we commend ourselves to every man's conscience in the sight of God (2 Cor. 4:2).

For the legislators to carry out honest supervision on the executive, they should wholeheartedly renounce deceptive and shameful ways, avoid distortion of God's Word and parliamentarian issues and set forth the truth plainly as they commend themselves to others' conscience before God and man. They must supervise the affairs of the executive in the very light of God's veracity.

Good governance, in the final analysis, is highly certain in the legislature in terms of the supervision of the executive if all the legislators embrace and cherish God's veracity and internalise it as the primary basis of their moral values. It is also possible if the legislators adopt divine veracity to be the only basis on which they are to carry out the supervision of the executive. Our world craves for honest legislators to exert their unbiased surveillance over the social and political affairs of the executives.

Can national parliament transform dishonest people and make them honest when working there? No, dishonest people make parliament dishonest, whereas honest people make it honest in the process of their operations therein. Then why send dishonest people to our national legislatures to supervise crucial affairs of our executives and expect good governance and moral values to prevail in our government systems? Let's get the right people to do the right job! But for us to realize sufficiently good governance in the legislature, it is good for us to also view it in the constitutional and appointive functions in the light of God's veracity.

Importance of Veracity in Constitutional and Appointive Functions

For the legislature to initiate amendments to the national constitution or participate fully in these changes, it should have good moral basis in terms of the divine veracity on which it operates. Also, this divine veracity will enable it to successfully carry out its appointive function. Obviously, when we talk about the divine veracity within the legislature, we expect that all men and women operating in the legislative system do embrace godly veracity as their guide, and that it is upon it that they base their moral values. We ought to understand that if that divine character is lacking, the legislators will not genuinely implement important constitutional and appointive functions.

In many instances, when members of parliament lack the spirit of God's veracity in their personal lives, they base their friendships and work on the actual basis of dishonesty. For instance, they dishonestly initiate additions or amendments to the national constitution or participate in such changes with the intention of achieving narrow interests at the expense of the national interests. Also, they yield themselves to the same spirit in endorsing or rejecting the appointment of key government officials or impeach the president for their wrong motive. And by doing so, they thrust their nation into a pool of moral injustice and corruption.

In order to carry out the constitutional and appointive functions honestly, the Lord wants the legislators to present things as they really are. Their veracity should reflect the fact that what they say can always be trusted. They should be honest in all situations. They must honestly execute their constitutional and appointive functions in the clear light of God's veracity.

It is good to note that good governance is only possible in the legislature when the legislature is marked by its being honest in dealing with the constitutional and appointive functions. It is also possible to speak of good governance in the legislature when all the people managing the legislative affairs wear the crown of the divine veracity as the fundamental foundation of their own personal character. It is the role of the general public to send credible people to national parliaments to execute these important tasks.

But if we want to see truly good governance in the legislative organ, all the legislative functions should also be guided by faithfulness, the last element of divine integrity.

Faithfulness

The Bible says, "Let love and faithfulness never leave you; bind them around your neck, write them on the tablet of your heart. Then you will win favour and a good name in the sight of God and man" (Prov. 3:3-4). Accordingly, the legislators are supposed to stick to the spirit of love and faithfulness as the basis for their ethical values and guiding mechanism for discharging their national obligations, like representation, law-making, public education, supervision of the executive, constitutional and appointive functions. As they sincerely follow this vital ethical code of conduct, they will certainly win favour and a good name in the eyes of God and man. But do our legislators really have favour and a good name before God and man? If not, why? Let us start the next section with the examination of good governance in the representation in the light of God's faithfulness.

Importance of Faithfulness in Representation

When representation is carried out in the wrong way, it results in serious conflicts between the parliamentary representatives and their constituents. In some instances. when members of the legislative assembly lack God's faithfulness in their own behaviour, their social and business relationships become unfaithful. In such cases, legislators do not represent the actual needs of their constituents before the legislative assembly. As such, it becomes quite difficult for the nation to understand and address people's needs on time. This misrepresentation of people's needs in parliament is one of the main reasons people do not realize their aspiration of having good governance in governments worldwide.

For the legislature to have proper representation, the constituents must exercise visual aptitude, watchful and keen mind and heart with a clear sense of moral maturity during the processes of national elections so as to avoid electing unfaithful persons to represent them in the legislative body. Noble duties should never ever be entrusted to faithless people because they will handle them dishonestly and cause suffering to those who are supposed to be represented.

But in case people seeking political office use their crooked means and become people's representatives, they still have these stern warnings and expectations from God and his moral beings; so legislators should take God's faithfulness as the guide for their individual moral values. God wants them to be faithful, proving true by keeping all their promises.

Guided by divine faithfulness, the legislators are able to represent the general aspirations of their voters in a good manner. They do not ignore the narrow or wider interests of their constituents. Also, because of their faithfulness, they are capable of retaining the confidence demonstrated by members of the public in choosing them to the high office. As they discharge this vital work faithfully, the legislators may entice the general public to emulate this divine faithfulness. Faithfulness is highly contagious. It is the reliable and strong glue that binds both the representatives and their constituents together and makes the role of representation worthwhile.

When faithful men and women execute legislative representation in the light of God's faithfulness, good governance automatically becomes the benchmark of the legislative system. In other words, when the general aspirations of all private and public sectors are fairly and loyally represented in the legislature by the legislators in the light of God's faithfulness, we can simply conclude that good governance exists in the legislature. It then becomes the reliable machinery with which the representation is carried out. Our world requires faithful legislative representatives who remain faithful to their words and promises under all circumstances. In order to avoid future regrets, let's staff our national parliaments with faithful men and women.

Nevertheless, in order for us to realise truly good governance in the legislature, the law-making process should also be guided by God's faithfulness.

Importance of Faithfulness in Law Making

Since the legislature deals with the formulation and enacting of laws as national statutes, it is imperative for it to wear the gown of the divine faithfulness in the eyes of the general public and in the eyes of the Lord, the Maker of the divine laws. Some of the international laws which are enacted by faithless men and women are really the cause of untold human miseries and God's wrath upon mankind because they serve some narrow, selfish interests of a few people at the expense of the general public. In other words, when faithless legislators make national laws, the spirit of their own faithlessness influences them to create laws that are unfaithful to the general public, especially the weak and the poor. For instance, the laws, though they bear the empty title of "the national laws", favour a few people but do not serve the interests of the majority of the citizens. They lack the essence of moral integrity.

Unfair laws produce nations where conflicts exist, where people oppress their fellow citizens. The oppressed citizens naturally respond by rebelling against their national governments, and of course, any national government that is at war with its own citizens should not exist.

Since unfair laws are destructive, the law-making process should be guided by godly faithfulness. And for the law-making process to be carried out faithfully, constituents must endeavour to nominate and elect people to the legislative assembly who base their lives and social and business relationships on the solid rock of biblical faithfulness. It is quite imperative that all the legislators make divine faithfulness as the guide for their moral values. They are to remain true in everything and keep all their promises as they formulate and enact statutes. They should not commit themselves on behalf of the whole nation to come up with laws that they will eventually regret having made or prove incapable to implement.

As a matter of fact, laws made in the light of God's faithfulness are, first and foremost, good in the eyes of the Lord. Also, they reflect the true aspirations of the general public, thus, vindicating those who made them. Genuine laws are made by the people for the people, and their making is guided by God's faithfulness. Such laws regard all the citizens as equal before God and man, and the spirit behind them is to have the whole nation existing as a unified entity, irrespective of geographical, racial, socio-economic, political and religious differences. Such laws create enabling environment, peace, brotherhood and national prosperity in the land.

It is good for us to note that good governance is only possible in the law-making process when all lawmakers completely embrace the divine faithfulness as the standard for their ethical values as they formulate and enact statutes. It is also possible only when the faithfulness of the lawmakers pervades the entire legislative system and makes it an oasis of the divine faithfulness. It is only when the law-making process is done in the light of God's faithfulness that we can genuinely speak of good governance in the legislature. We must not permit faithless people to make our laws! However, good governance in the legislature will still be incomplete until it is also visible in public education.

Importance of Faithfulness in Public Education

Who can really place his trust in a faithless person? A faithless person may not even trust himself! As previously explained, public education is one of the most significant functions of the legislature. It is the process by which the legislature keeps the general public abreast of crucial, socio-economic and political issues.

Very often, when this noble legislative function is not done loyally, especially when the legislators do not keep their words, saying one thing but doing the other, this creates some mistrust or unfaithfulness between the legislature and the general public. And such unfaithfulness becomes a thorn in the flesh in the legislature. The result is an unhealthy environment for the existence of good governance.

In fact, national legislative matters are closely connected to the lives of the people and their collective and individual possessions. They also affect national sovereignty and the nation's general aspirations. Considering the significance of these matters and more other pertinent legislative issues, their discussions and deliberations in the eyes and the ears of the public must be done in faithful and honourable ways. Sacred matters are shouldered by faithful and sacred gentlemen and ladies—the men and women of unquestionable moral integrity.

By nominating and electing faithless people as legislators, constituents are merely putting the people they elect to moral test; as a result, they let themselves and their entire nation down. Since deviant legislators will certainly fail to deliver in the end, they fail themselves, fail their constituents and fail their whole nation. They become wrong people in the right places. Most of our world legislative assemblies, particularly in the Third World countries, are, unfortunately, mostly staffed by faithless men and women.

For the legislature to carry out the public education role faithfully, the men and women working in it must uphold divine faithfulness as the keystone upon which they base their moral values. Constituents are to make sure that the people they send to national assemblies are of un-doubtful faithfulness. As they discuss crucial social and political matters in parliament, they should prove true by keeping all their promises or words. They must emulate God's faithfulness.

Subsequently, their faithfulness should permeate the entire legislative system, causing it to become an enabling environment for proper public education. Our world not only needs rhetorical and candid legislators but also faithful representatives who can carry out the public education role of the legislature in the light of God's faithfulness.

When the legislators excel in being faithful in the discussion of vital national issues by being accountable for whatever they say and carrying out their debates in the light of God's faithfulness, we can comfortably speak of good governance in the public education process in the legislature. Let's entrust legislative public education role to faithful citizens! However, we cannot talk of truly good governance in the legislature if it is not carrying out its role of the supervision of the executive faithfully.

Importance of Faithfulness in the Supervision of Executive

Because of the importance of the supervisory role of the legislature on the activities of the executive, it is imperative that the legislature adopts God's faithfulness as its guide in executing this vital function.

Let me start the discussion with the following soul-searching questions: If you are really not faithful in deed, word and thought, can you expect or require me to be faithful? Are you one of the naive guys who demand others to do what they say but not what they do?

It is quite impossible, of course, for an unfaithful person to exercise supervision on someone else's activities. One needs to be absolutely clean before carrying out any good surveillance on someone else's moral issues. Faithful examiners only involve themselves with subjects that are in accordance with their particular field of expertise. Or else, they cannot completely differentiate between good and bad.

Very often, faithless legislators execute this vital legislative function on the national affairs of the executive organ. And lack of moral integrity in their personal lives blinds them from differentiating what is morally correct from what is ethically wrong. In other words, they are unable to identify the problems and suggest practical solutions to them. Nor are they able to provide admonitions in the executive system. As such, their supervision on the executive ends up causing more damage than good to the executive organ of the government and to the whole nation.

For the legislature to exert fair and faithful supervisory exercise on the executive, first and foremost, the legislators must be men and women who are chosen after careful examination in respect of their ethical behaviour, especially their faithfulness. If people who fall short are chosen, the entire legislature as well as the whole nation will be thrust into jeopardy.

Legislators ought to imitate God's faithfulness as the primary guide for their moral code of conduct. In every condition, they ought to prove true and keep all their promises. To carry out their work faithfully, the Lord does not want the legislators to make their promises thoughtlessly. And in the event that they promise somethings, they should remain faithful to them because their faithfulness is critical for the betterment of the whole nation. The importance of having faithful legislatures to carry out the supervision of the executive cannot be overstated.

Good governance is possible in the supervision of the

executive only when the legislature embraces God's faithfulness as one of the unique marks of its operation. Only then is it qualified to supervise the activities of the executive.

Supervision of any kind is prone to bias on the part of the supervisor unless it is done by one who is guided by godly faithfulness. So let faithful legislature perform fair and faithful supervision of the executive with only the aim of achieving the common good of mankind and God's own glory as well. Nonetheless, good governance can still be lacking in the legislature if the constitutional and appointive functions are not carried out in the light of God's faithfulness.

Importance of Faithfulness in Constitutional and Appointive Functions

Any legislative system cannot fairly carry out constitutional and appointive functions unless it uses God's faithfulness as the benchmark by which these vital roles are measured. All additions and amendments to the national constitution as well as any ratification of international treaties require the undivided attention of faithful men and women whose moral values are completely submerged in the clear river of God's faithfulness. Also, for the appointive function to be a blessing to the nation, it should also be exercised by equally faithful parliamentarians.

Unfortunately, most of the constitutional and appointive functions are not done in good faith for the benefit of the state but for the common good of the few parliamentarians as they seek to serve narrow interests. The result is complete downfall of the entire nation.

For example, when such legislators initiate additions or amendments to the national constitution or participate in such changes, they do so with the hidden agenda of achieving their secret goals. They can also approve or reject the appointments of certain key civil servants, not for the common good of the country but just to meet their selfish goals. Such faithless legislators can even impeach the president when he seems to threaten their narrow aspirations.

In order to implement constitutional and appointive functions in the proper manner for the common good of the whole nation, people should elect to the national assembly men and women who constantly wear God's faithfulness as their attire and are known for acceptable social and business relationships. People in most parts of the world keep crying over the conduct of their faithless legislators, but what they fail to understand is that people reap what they sow. Therefore, let's ensure that we send faithful men and women to our legislative assemblies so as to have faithful legislatures and faithful nations.

The Lord expects legislators to emulate His faithfulness as the guide for their moral character. Their faithfulness should mean that they prove true and keep their promises under every circumstance. In the process of performing these constitutional and appointive roles, the legislators are not supposed to give their words thoughtlessly. They are to remain faithful in whatever they say because their words or promises have consequences from the Lord and their fellow human beings.

Good governance is possible in the legislature only when the legislative system is known for being faithful in handling both small and big legislative matters. Once more, good governance is possible in the legislature only when its constitutional and appointive functions are handled by faithful men and women. It is naïve to speak of good governance in the unfaithful legislative system where constitutional and appointive functions are carried out with some ulterior or ill motives by parliamentarians. God wants the faithful to carry out these vital roles.

On the whole, the legislature urgently needs faithful men and women to carry out crucial amendments to the constitution or fully participate in such noble changes. Also, they are to ratify any international treaty done by the president on behalf of the state and fairly approve or reject the appointment of some key government officials. If things are done in broad daylight, good governance will surely takeover from bad governance and chronic moral corruption. We can honestly and faithfully speak of the presence of good governance in the legislative system only when all the key functions—representation, law-making, public education, supervision of the executive, constitutional and appointive functions—are done by faithful men and women in the light of God's faithfulness.

Above all, when legislators base their personal behaviour and legislative functions on all the three elements of moral integrity—genuineness, veracity and faithfulness—good moral values and good governance get leeway to flourish in national legislatures in particular and whole governments in general. If we want to experience continuous good governance and acceptable ethical values in our nations, then it is our sole national and moral duty to staff our national legislatures with men and women who are known for genuineness, veracity and faithfulness, the three elements of moral integrity.

But truly good governance will be lacking in the legislative organ of the government unless all the legislative functions are also submerged in the clear river of divine love, the last element of moral quality. That is the primary focus of the following chapter.

Chapter 6
Love in the Legislature

Since the parliament is where the fate of the nation and its individuals is determined, protected, upheld and cherished, I wish to begin by drawing the reader to the following short passage of Scripture:

> Anyone who claims to be in the light but hates his brother is still in the darkness. Whoever loves his brother lives in the light, and there is nothing in him to make him stumble. But whoever hates his brother is in the darkness and walks around in the darkness; he does not know where he is going, because the darkness has blinded him. Dear friends, let us love one another, for love comes from God. Everyone who loves has been born of God and knows God (1 Jn. 2:9-11, 4:7).

The Lord expects legislators to walk in the light and love other members of the public as themselves. If they refuse to love their brothers and sisters, they are not born of God and cannot claim to know Him. In that case, they are in the darkness and walk around in the darkness at the risk of stumbling and falling terribly with the entire nation. Do we need legislators who know the Lord, love their brothers and sisters and walk in the light for the common good of the people and for God's own glory, or do we want to see our legislatures controlled by loveless men and women who do not know God, hate their brothers and sisters and grope in the darkness of corruption and thus, exposing our people to danger and the wrath of the Lord upon the nation?

The purpose of this section is to examine how good governance can be achieved when all the legislative functions—representation, law-making, public education, supervision of the executive, constitutional and appointive functions—are carried out in the broad light of the four elements of love: benevolence, grace, mercy and persistence. Let's begin by seeing how benevolence can enhance good governance in the legislature.

Benevolence

Benevolent legislators promote the spirit of divine benevolence in their nation. Such nations become kind and hence lovable states. The result is God's blessing to the citizens who begin to live and operate in the shadow of God's love.

But when unkind men and women occupy and control the national legislatures, they make their nations unkind and oppressive to their own people. As a result, people live and operate outside God and His love.

Under this section I shall bathe all the functions of the legislature in the pool of the divine benevolence to see how it can facilitate the essence of good governance in and outside the premises of the legislature. Now let me discuss below the possibility of having good governance in the legislature's role of representation in the light of God's benevolence.

Importance of Benevolence in Representation

As already established, representation is one of the basic functions of the legislature whereby members represent various sectors of the population in the national parliament. Such sectors include both private and public interests. The legislators are expected to represent fairly these private and public aspirations before parliament. But when the representation is not done well, the constituents feel betrayed by their representatives. When this occurs, constituents lose faith in their representatives.

It is common knowledge that no one can genuinely serve and represent people he does not truly love. In the same way, people cannot love and follow someone who does not love them. So when the legislative house is full of men and women who lack God's benevolence in their own lives, accordingly, their social and business relationships lack the spirit of divine benevolence. The result is an unhealthy representation.

Unhealthy representation means poor relationship between the constituents and their representatives. Under such circumstances, the legislators lack genuine benevolence of God to enable them to love the members of their constituencies as they love themselves. And when they fail to represent their people benevolently, the general public responds in the same way by not being kind to them and to the legislature in general. Naturally, unkind legislators make the legislature unkind to itself, to its government and to the entire public. In the same manner, the citizens become unkind to the legislature as well as to the entire government.

In order for fair representation to exist, it is the duty of voters to critically appraise vote seekers so as to send to parliament good and benevolent representatives. Failure to that, they will be to blame when they find their legislatures manned by bad and mean legislators.

The Lord expects the legislators to embrace God's benevolence as the guide upon which to base their moral values. Their divine code of conduct will prompt them to seek unselfishly the welfare of their constituents because doing this is in line with

God's love. Besides meeting the interests of those they love, the legislators are also compelled to care for the aspirations of those who hate them because this is in accordance with God's desire (Matt. 5:45). Above all, the legislators are required by the Lord to protect the general wellbeing of all subhuman creatures.

Good governance in representation is only possible within and outside the legislature when all men and women working as legislators fully cherish the divine benevolence as the benchmark of their moral values and through which to carry out their work. It is only when the aspirations of all the sectors of the population, including subhuman creatures, are fairly represented before the national parliament that we can speak of the existence of good governance in the legislature. Legislatures need men and women who can unwaveringly stand for the interests of others. Let compassionate men and women always stand for others in our national assemblies, for such are people-centred, ready to cry with those who cry and laugh with those who laugh.

But good governance would be incomplete in the legislature, despite the presence of fair representation, if law-making is not also carried out in the clear light of God's benevolence. The purpose of the next section is, therefore, to discuss the role of benevolence in law-making.

Importance of Benevolence in Law Making

The parliamentarians sometimes carry out their role of making the law with a lot of bias. For example, they favour certain parts of the population while marginalising others. Subsequently, the laws made through these unfair procedures are partial and tend to cause destruction in the nation.

Normally, the goal of national laws is to safeguard the common interests of both the foes and friends as well as the aspirations of subhuman creatures living within the national boundaries. This is so because God lets His sun shine on both good and bad people (Matt. 5:45) and takes absolute care of all the subhuman creatures (Matt. 6:26, 28, 10:29). So state laws are to take into consideration the protection of the national environment, for the Psalmist says, "You open your hand and satisfy the desires of every living thing" (Ps. 145:16). Even soldiers were to desist from destroying fruit trees. God warns people against unnecessary destruction of the environment, even in times of conflict (Deut. 20:19-20) because He is the Creator, and all creatures look up to Him to provide for them. The environment is an expression of God's benevolence, and it should be treated with respect, though not to be worshipped. The Bible contains much about the importance of taking care of the environment, for example in Gen. 1:26-30, 2:15.

Laws made by those who lack God's benevolence in their individual lives tend to be oppressive. They do not promote true love in individuals or even in the nation. For instance, they discriminate against certain people, preventing the weak and the poor from enjoying the benefits of justice. That is, they alienate some people and favour others. Also, such laws do not encourage taking care of the environment. They do not consider and safeguard the common welfare of other creatures like birds, marine life and animals. Such unkind laws end up fomenting civil strife within and outside the national borders.

So for the legislature to enact just national statutes that safeguard the aspirations of the entire populace, including other subhuman creatures, God's benevolence must be the fundamental guide for all their activities. Because of the importance of the law-making process, God expects all the legislators to embrace His divine benevolence as the benchmark of their moral character and proper machinery by which they are to execute their national activities.

While debating laws and eventually enacting them as

statutes, the legislators are to be unselfishly guided by the desire to improve the welfare of the general public. They must make sure that the laws they make reflect the selflessness of divine love. But for the nation to get benevolent legislators in its legislature, the constituents are duty-bound to select or elect men and women of unquestionable moral behaviour to be their representatives. The kind, loving God has made benevolent laws to show His nature and also for the benefit of His creatures, especially mankind; hence, we too should be kind and loving citizens by enacting laws that take into account the welfare of others as well as for the glory of our Creator.

God is happy when legislators play out their divine benevolence by demonstrating their affection towards the citizens by minding their welfare. God's benevolence is shown by caring and providing for those He loves and even for the ones who hate Him. Moreover, when national laws take national interests into consideration, the general public own them as their own laws and as being above everybody, including the president. This benevolence will saturate the whole nation for the goodness of all the national creatures, for God decrees: 'Be fruitful and increase in number; fill the earth and subdue it. Rule over the fish of the sea and the birds of the air and over every living creature that moves on the ground' (Gen. 1:28).

For truly good governance to exist in the law-making function of the legislature, all laws must satisfy the desires of every living thing, including birds and fish, among others. So when law-making is based on the divine benevolence so as to protect the entire interests of all citizens and other subhuman creatures within the national borders, we can comfortably say that good governance is in existence in the law-making process. Such impartial laws are the ground on which good governance stands for the general welfare of mankind and also for the glory of God.

Yet apart from the evidence of the divine benevolence in the execution of the parliamentary representation and law-making, we cannot really speak of the existence of truly good governance in the legislature if the same is absent in the public education function of the legislature.

Importance of Benevolence in Public Education

As already established, public education is one of the vital roles of the legislature. But when the legislators approach important deliberations with selfish motives, the general public is denied access to the truth, receiving doctored information. Yet wrong information is as dangerous as a gun in the wrong hands in the midst of the public. For if the legislature debates some vital national issues, not in the clear light of love and kindness but with selfish and ill intentions, it will in effect be misinforming citizens. If they assume that they got the right information from their parliamentarians, people could innocently take wrong steps relating to socio-economic and political lines and end up suffering. Of course, it will take longer for the legislature to correct such a mistake in an effort to protect the public, even when there is the will to do it, for it is not always easy to err and correct the error in time before damage occurs.

A politically and economically misinformed population easily lose faith in the legislature and the entire government. And how do you expect a government that has lost the trust of its citizens to exist and perform smoothly? Our legislatures now face this big challenge of miscommunication in direct violation of the vital function of public education.

Hence, legislators must be very careful with what they say and how they say it while discussing crucial social and political matters in the hearing of the general public. For the legislature to carry out the right public education, the prerequisite is that all the national constituents carefully nominate or elect people who demonstrate the spirit of moral benevolence in their code of conduct to represent them in the national legislative forums. Moreover, people are not sent to parliament to warm chairs as they look for ways to address their narrow interests at the expense of the national goals but to safeguard and promote the national image for the common good of all. So it is the noble duty of the voters to send to parliament those who have demonstrated godly benevolence in their lives to be their legislators. Of course, you can't honestly term a person that lacks moral benevolence in his life: "honourable member" as people nowadays mistakenly do.

Legislators should adopt God's benevolence as the guide for their ethical values. Then these refined values can saturate the entire legislative structure, enabling it to deliberate on national matters and carry out the public education in the light of God's benevolence. While debating national issues in the legislative assembly, the legislators should avoid any hidden agenda to enrich themselves and instead unselfishly seek the welfare of the entire population. For when they do so, legislators reflect the self-sacrifice that characterizes divine love. Instead of undermining the interests of their constituents through hidden agenda, they should give them proper public education in the light of God's benevolence. A kind and compassionate person imparts knowledge and information to others with openness.

To recap this section, good governance in the public education is only possible when all men and women operating in the legislative system embrace divine benevolence, and it becomes a recognisable mark of their ethical values. When this divine virtue permeates the entire legislative structure and becomes the machinery with which to carry out deliberations in parliament with the eventual aim of giving the right information to the members of the public, then we can then be justified to conclude that good governance is in existence in the legislature.

We cannot, however, talk of truly good governance in the legislature if the supervision of the executive is not guided by godly benevolence. The focus of the following section is to examine the role of good governance in the supervision of the executive in the light of godly benevolence.

Importance of Benevolence in Supervision of Executive

As shown earlier, one of the most important functions of the legislature is conducting close watch over the affairs of the executive. But, unfortunately, when the parliamentarians who have ill feelings towards those working in the executive branch of the government become involved in this important role of the legislature, the results can be disastrous. This is because the legislators will not play the role of a fair watchdog because their eyes are blinded by selfish, secret motives. In fact, when members of the legislative assembly lack benevolence in their character, they supervise the national affairs of the executive organ in the unkindly manner of bullies. Their intentions will not be to look for errors and see how to help the executive correct them but to punish the officials concerned. Certainly, there is nothing wrong with warning or even punishing culprits, but the primary purpose for supervision is to maintain proper checks and balances within the executive.

The moment it becomes clear that the purpose of the supervisory function of the legislature is to humiliate and punish people within the executive and not to help them correct mistakes and improve the system, the executive will refuse to cooperate and start to fight back the legislature. This situation will result in unnecessary tension between the two parties as well as in the entire nation. Thus, this vital legislative function will be rendered ineffective and the whole nation will suffer. Do you see this unhealthy situation occurring in your country's legislature? If so, who do you think is to blame?

Of course, the first ones to blame, if there is need to apportion blame, are the constituents who brought these non-benevolent legislators into power. The legislative assembly is not there to reform moral deviants. It should be occupied by those known for moral excellence so as to use it to reform the general public while they are in power. Thus, for you to see and hear your parliament exercising successfully its noble function of supervising the executive, you have the inescapable obligation to send to it men and women who clothe themselves with God's benevolence.

On the whole, in order for the legislators to exercise fairness in their supervision of the executive, God expects them to embrace His divine benevolence as a recognisable aspect of their moral character. This divine virtue will help them establish some cordial relationship with those working in the executive. And on the basis of that relationship, they are likely to carry out supervisory role on the executive appropriately. To put it differently, while executing this significant role, the legislators are to unselfishly seek the wellbeing of the whole public, including those who are being supervised. This act will demonstrate the self-sacrificial quality of divine love. It is in order for us to note here that as they carry out their fair surveillance, parliamentarians should overlook personal differences between them and those operating in the executive if they are to excel in their supervision role of the executive. This is because such differences can overshadow the lenses of any vital equipment used in this surveillance by the legislature, and, tragically, the end result will not favour any party within the whole nation. Legislators need to be clear-sighted while they carry out their supervisory task on the executive organ. They are to be free to supervise and correct any possible mistakes benevolently, not punishing the culprits as if they are the worst people under the sun but rather as people who deserve kindness in the course of their reform process.

It is only when supervision of the executive by the legislature is guided by godly benevolence for the general welfare of the entire public that we can say that good governance exists in the legislature. Only then is the legislature a favourable environment for the practice of good governance in the government.

Nonetheless, we can still not talk of the existing of good governance in the legislature if the legislators do not implement constitutional and appointive functions in the light of God's benevolence.

Importance of Benevolence in Constitutional and Appointive Functions

When legislators fairly initiate additions and amendments to the national constitution or participate in such changes and honestly consider for ratification of international treaties in which the state president has involved himself on behalf of the nation and the whole nation is happy with the outcome, we can say that the parliamentarians have done a noble job for the benefit of the general public. In the same manner, if they approve or reject the appointments of certain key government officials, not because they hate or dislike them but rather for the welfare of the general public, then we can speak of there being the essence of good governance in the legislature.

However, this is not usually the case because the legislators sometimes exercise their constitutional and appointive functions with the aim of serving their own narrow interests. These hidden motives tend to create some deep holes underneath the government, pushing it to tremble and fall terribly. For instance, in the event that the legislators do not base their moral character and social and business relationships on the divine benevolence, they tend to carry out these functions in an unkind manner by initiating some additions and amendments to the national constitution or participating in these changes fully, not with the aim of uplifting their nation up but to bring it down to her knees in the process of serving their own selfish desires. Similarly, they could impeach an important person or persons or approve or reject the appointment of some key government officials just to meet their narrow interests at the expense of others and national aspirations.

Is it good for politicians to let their nation down as they seek to realize their individual aspirations at the expense of national goals? Would their constituents and God be happy with them? How can they extricate themselves out of the mess and save their nation?

These vital legislative roles cannot bear fruit within and outside the boundaries of our nations unless they are executed compassionately by people who are renowned for their love of others. But how can we get such legislators who wear divine benevolence as their recognisable necklace?

As we seek to answer this question, let us know that such rare men and women are just sitting in our midst. We know who they are. They may not even be well known or rich; yet they exist among us. And it is our sole responsibility to identify or elect to political office those with undeniable moral benevolence and send them to man and influence our legislative assemblies for the good of mankind and for God's glory. The moment we decide to send selfish people to represent us and the entire nation in the national assembly, that is tantamount to inviting personal and national problems and God's curse.

Also, in order to avoid this unpleasant state of affairs in our nation, our legislature should embrace God's divine benevolence as the cornerstone upon which its policies and guiding principles are based. In other words, God wants all parliamentarians to wear the gown of the divine benevolence as a clear mark of their moral values. As they exercise their constitutional and appointive functions, they must unselfishly seek the ultimate welfare of the whole nation, including its good neighbourliness with other nations. They must also make sure that such international treaties are mutually inclusive and the welfare of each party considered in drawing the agreements. That is, they should be guided by godly benevolence for the welfare of all the parties involved. Also, the approval or rejection of the appointments or even the impeachment of any key government official should reflect the selflessness of the legislators.

I conclude by saying that good governance in the constitutional and appointive functions of the legislature exists when all the men and women working in the legislature wear the mantle of the divine benevolence as the basic standard of their moral character and the guide for discharging their legislative constitutional and appointive roles in the light of God's benevolence. Also, we can only speak without shame of the presence of good governance in respect of the constitutional and appointive functions of the legislature if the divine benevolence of the legislators becomes the cornerstone of the legislative system and when it becomes evident in the whole government. When that happens, the legislators become the real salt and light of the world in terms of good governance.

We cannot speak of the presence of good governance in the legislature unless the representation, law-making, public education, supervision of the executive and constitutional and appointive functions of the legislature are fairly implemented, guided by God's benevolence. Also, we can only talk of good governance in the legislature when it has completely engulfed the entire spectrum of the government. Let all the men and women working within the legislative system firmly uphold the divine benevolence as a recognisable mark of their moral character.

Nevertheless, the truly good governance in the legislature will still not have been achieved unless all the functions of the legislature conform to divine grace, the second element of God's love.

Grace

The primary focus of this section of Chapter Six is to examine the way in which the whole legislature can adopt divine grace as the cornerstone of its operations. We cannot actually talk of the essence of good governance in the legislature in the light of the divine grace unless it is evident in the representation, law-making, public education, supervision of the executive, constitutional and appointive functions of the legislature.

Importance of Grace in Representation

Graceless legislators have no grace towards one another, do not show grace to their constituents and do not show grace to the executive organ or any other important branch of the government or fellow human beings. Their social and business relationship is not built around God's love. In most instances, they treat and relate to their voters in unloving and inconsiderate manner, not treating them as the people who love them and sponsored them to the legislative assembly.

In the end, the legislators' failure to be grateful creates division between those who are represented and their representatives and the attendant loss of confidence in the legislature and the entire government. What will ensue if the masses fail to trust their government and thus, cease to cooperate with it? Although it may not collapse immediately, it will henceforth be a government of the few, by the few and for the few.

For us to have effective and efficient representation in the legislature, all the constituents should be careful during the general elections to glean people with good moral values, especially in the area of the divine grace, and send them to the national assembly as their honourable representatives. That is the way to pre-empt future embarrassment which may occur in the course of the legislative representation. When it comes to moral goodness, there are no shortcuts; there is no magic formula, for only the right people can make things right.

Hence, it would be fine for all men and women working within the legislative structures to attach importance to divine grace and take it as the solid standard of their ethical character. That way, legislators will represent the various interests of their constituents graciously. Nor should representation be guided by the merit of those being represented; rather, it should be guided by their individual needs.

When the legislature bases its representation on the divine grace alone, the entire public takes the actual ownership of the legislative assembly because it safeguards their interests. Such a fair and gracious representation is what God expects from any legislature, for He opens His hand and satisfies the desire of every living thing (Ps. 145: 16).

Our world is deeply in need of gracious parliamentarians who are guided by divine grace to represent the interests of their people in the legislature. Even if I did not vote for you during the elections, your divine grace as my parliamentarian will compel you to overlook that and represent me graciously, just the way God overlooked our sins and went on with the plan of saving us.

Good governance, when it comes to representation, is only achievable when the legislature embraces divine grace as its guide and by which it graciously exercises its representation. To put it in another way, when the legislature fairly and graciously represents the aspirations of all, including those of subhuman creatures, then we can speak of real good governance in the legislature that is guided by God's grace. Let gracious people represent us in our parliaments!

But in order for us to have truly good governance in the legislature in the light of God's grace, its law-making function must also be carried out with God's grace.

Importance of Grace in Law-Making

There is no single person on the face of the earth who does not require the grace of God in their daily life. This is because people are by nature prone to stumbling and falling. So the whole of human race is sinful and badly needs divine grace, as is clear from the following Scripture: "For all have sinned and fall short of the glory of God, and are justified freely by his grace through the redemption that came by Christ Jesus" (Rom. 3:23-24).

While the Lord offered His Son, our Lord and Saviour Jesus Christ, as the atonement for our sins, He did justice without compromising His love. God's justice and His love are never in conflict. They are ever in harmony, to the extent where Erickson said, "Actually, love and justice have worked together in God's dealing with man. God's justice requires that there be payment of the penalty for sin. God's love, however, desires man to be restored to fellowship with him."[13]

Since national laws are the worthy yardsticks for divine justice, they must be based on the divine grace. To stretch this explanation further, the real meaning of the interpretation and the application of the divine justice is to eventually restore the offender in the process. That is why the presence of the divine grace in law-making is vital. Laws are not meant to destroy people but to change them for good and restore them back into society for the betterment of mankind and for God's glory.

---

13 Ibid., Erickson, 298.

Conversely, national laws that lack the will of the divine grace tend to be harsh despite being professional. They do not exist for the welfare of anybody—including the lawmakers themselves—and they end up alienating people from their government. Repressive laws do not consider the interest of sub-human creatures or the necessary coexistence for harmony in the environment. Also, they are against good neighbourliness when it comes to relating with other nations. This sometimes throws the nation into unnecessary conflicts with her neighbours as well as with herself—local communities fighting among themselves or against their own government. We normally see and hear about such legislative assemblies, especially in the Third World countries. How can we prevent such legislative debacle from happening?

If we really want to see laws with a human face in them and which also respect and protect other creatures, their primary architects must be men and women who base their moral code of conduct and social and business friendships on the solid rock of God's grace. They must be people who hurt when others hurt and rejoice when others rejoice, not people who shed crocodile tears when others are in pain.

But do we have such humane people among us? We definitely do because good and bad people live side by side under the sun. So it is just a matter of time, patience and sincerity on the part of the constituents and they identify and send gracious men and women as their representatives in the national assembly. If the necessary precaution is taken in each and every constituency—and done in good time—our global legislatures will be overflowing with real honourable members who will make good and gracious laws for the welfare of mankind, for the general good of other creatures and also for God's glory.

Hence, our legislators, even if they are graceless in their moral conduct, badly need divine and gracious guidance to help them interpret and apply the legal statutes properly. Just as the God has extended to us His grace by the atoning death of His Son Jesus Christ, He expects each and every one of us to extend the same grace to others. God expects all the legislators to embrace His divine grace as the foundation on which they are to build their moral values. If they become morally good, their divine grace will saturate the entire legislature and make it conducive for law-making exercises that are guided by God's grace. For instance, while debating and enacting national laws, the legislators must not only view members of the public on the basis of their merit but also on the basis of their apparent desire to enact laws.

Good governance in the law-making function of the legislature is only possible when all deliberations that eventually lead to the enacting of laws into state statutes are carried out by gracious legislators, guided by God's grace. But apart from good governance both in the representation and in the law-making functions in the light of God's grace, it is also important to have it in the public education.

Importance of Grace in Public Education

While debating legislative issues, sometimes politicians go for each other's throat like ungracious chickens fighting over territorial domain. Their aim is to protect their narrow interests. As a result, parliament becomes like a slaughter house, which is full of political casualties whose self-esteem has been wounded beyond repair. The house also becomes a graceless environment for showing off, acting foolish, jealousy, envy, hatred and egocentrism.

In fact, it is unfortunate to note that some legislative forums are just like cinema halls where people watch, hear and learn all kinds of bad manners. Graceless legislators take advantage of such an unhealthy environment to influence and split members of the public as they seek their support instead of giving them proper public education. In other words, when the legislators are not gracious with themselves, they will not educate the general public in a gracious manner but will, instead, create groupings among the members of the same nation that are hostile to each other. Are you familiar with such embarrassing and inhumane situations that are caused by the legislature?

For us to make our legislative houses as places for true honourable members, real gentlemen and gentle ladies, our respective national constituencies must all the time identify and elect men and women whose moral behaviour and social and business relationships as individuals are thoroughly submerged in and bathed with the clean spirit of God's grace. Failure to that, we should be always prepared and willing to live with and endure graceless national assemblies and their unpleasant consequences. We must be prepared to reap what we sow without pointing any insincere finger of blame towards others, including the graceless legislators.

For us to realise the presence of truly good governance in the legislature so far as public education is concerned, all the legislators must embrace the divine grace as the cornerstone of their moral character and through which they are to channel all their lengthy parliamentary debates of socio-economic and political significance.

When parliamentary debates are done in the light of God's grace and hence, reflect a human face, the general public learns a good lesson from the conduct of their politicians. This in turn enables them to live in the same light of God's grace as they interact with each other on a day-to-day basis. It is the duty of the legislature to carry out honest public education among its own citizens.

Our legislative assemblies need men and women who wear the clear lenses of the divine grace through which they are to view political and socio-economic issues that are being discussed. It is by God's grace that Jesus Christ came and died for our sins, and we too need to show loving kindness to one another.

Therefore, good governance in the public education is possible only when the legislature takes God's grace as its recognisable benchmark with which to measure the accuracy and fairness of the way debates are conducted in parliament. Again, it is possible only when the masses get the correct and therefore, transforming information from the legislative assembly.

But besides that, it is also good for us to see the role of grace in the legislature's supervision of the executive and its contribution to good governance.

Importance of Grace in the Supervision of the Executive

Supervision of the activities of the executive should be done carefully, fairly and graciously by applying public relations techniques in the correct manner. In case of any issue concerning the executive, the best approach should be for the legislature to look at the problem objectively without seeing the people in the executive as the problem. It should be de-linked from them. The reason why it should be handled with maximum care is to avoid any sort of political instability in case the executive retaliates aggressively. The primary aim of the executive supervision is to graciously and honestly identify both the errors of omission as well as the errors of commission that may occur when the executive is discharging its duty. The legislature ought to graciously and meticulously de-link such mistakes from the personnel in the executive and address them within the framework of national interest. Normally, this supervisory exercise is a reformatory measure that is meant to provide an opportunity to rebuke those responsible and restore certain order in line with God's grace and as guided by the national constitution.

Unfortunately, this is not always the case. Very often, when an ungracious legislature carries out its supervisory function on the executive, resentments tend to develop between the executive and the legislature. This is because the legislators' gracelessness towards members of the executive takes over and spoils the exercise. Members of the legislature come in hurry, not to identify the problem and provide possible solutions to the problem but just to name, shame and punish sternly those associated with it. In such a case, an unworthy strife involving the two parties tends to follow and eventually makes the government to stand on shaky ground, propped by wrestlers.

In order for the legislature to execute its supervisory function on the executive honestly and satisfactorily, voters should make sure that their representatives to the national assembly are people known for their graciousness. We should, however, point out that being gracious in character does not mean being unconcerned, poor administrator or accommodative of evil doers. Really, what it means is that one is caring and loving like God and is able to approach and address personal, social and national issues through the lenses of the divine love. It helps one to deal with life's day-to-day matters seriously but lovingly.

The moment we remove God's grace from our lives, that is the moment we remove the presence of love as well as the loving Lord, the only source of the genuine love, from our lives. Let our legislatures be peopled by gracious men and women. God expects all the legislators to embrace His divine grace as the basis for their ethical character and by which they are to implement and evaluate their supervision of the executive.

While supervising the executive activities, the legislators should not only deal with those working in the executive on the basis of their status but on the basis of their needs. The legislators should demonstrate love, goodness, generosity and expertise so as to carry out fairly and honestly surveillance activities over the affairs of the executive for the general good of the entire nation.

It is only when the operations of the legislature are completely guided by divine grace should we speak of proper supervision of the executive. But for truly good governance to exist in the legislature in the light of God's grace, it is also imperative for the constitutional and appointive functions to be carried out in the light of God's grace.

Importance of Grace in Constitutional and Appointive Functions

Part of the Lord's Prayer says, "Forgive us our debts, as we have also forgiven our debtors" (Matt. 6:12). And Jesus Christ in expoundig this says, "For if you forgive men when they sin against you, your heavenly Father will also forgive you. But if you do not forgive men their sins, your Father will not forgive your sins" (Matt.6:14-15).

For our legislators to avoid unnecessary quarrels with other people, especially those in the executive and the judiciary, and in order for them to execute their important legislative roles unhindered, they should embrace the attitude of forgiveness, guided by divine grace.

It is an undeniable fact that these important functions cannot be done well by the legislators in the absence of the divine grace in their hearts and souls. For instance, if they are not graciously imbued with God's love, the legislators will merely initiate additions and amendments or participate actively in such changes with the aim of punishing their political opponents in one way or the other. Also, because of their ulterior motives, the ungracious parliamentarians may approve or reject the appointment of or impeach certain government officials just to punish them.

In most cases, our legislators execute these vital roles in a graceless manner. For instance, they are quick to initiate some additions or amendments to the national constitution just to take care of their shallow interests at the expense of the welfare of the general public. They follow the same trend when it comes to carrying out the appointive function. Sometimes, graceless legislators impeach their national president not because of any known wrongdoing but simply because he prevents them from carrying out some malpractices that have the underlying objective of realizing selfish goals. Does this ever happen in your country's legislative assembly?

In order to see our legislators implement these important roles of the constitutional and appointive functions in a gracious and rightful manner, it is our unavoidable duty to deliberately seek among ourselves men and women who base their personal behaviour and social and business relationships on the divine grace and vote them to office in the legislative assembly. We should not expect graceless and loveless legislators to carry out important national functions; instead, we should expect them to put first their own interests ahead of national interests.

We, the national voters, can save ourselves and our nations a lot of heartache associated with corruption while at the same time promoting good governance simply by sending only those with good moral values to our national legislative assemblies. Actually, this is what people in the Western World and other advanced nations do, and that is why their legislative assemblies are full of people who have high moral ethics. It is the high time we too applied this secret for the improvement of our own welfare. If you want to reap shame and disgrace, let immoral people represent your interests!

If the legislature bases its constitutional and appointive

functions on the divine grace, the Lord and all the nationals will be happy with the good work done by this organ. This is simply because people will see fairness in what is done by the legislature as it deals with national matters, not maliciously targeting certain people with punitive laws. In such a healthy legislative environment, government appointments are not approved or turned down by the parliamentarians on the basis of individual grudges but for the welfare of people. These gracious laws bridge the gap between members of parliament and the rest of the people. Hence, they will inevitably bring peace and harmony within and outside the national borders.

To bring this discussion to a conclusion, good governance in the constitutional and appointive functions is possible only when legislators initiate additions and amendments to constitution, not to benefit supposedly important people but to address the needs of all. The other indicator of good governance is when the legislators approve or reject the appointment of certain people to certain positions in government, not because of personal differences but for the sake of the welfare of the nation. It is only when legislators are guided by their own goodness and generosity in discharging their duties related to the constitutional and appointive functions can we say that good governance is evident in the constitutional and appointive functions as guided by God's grace.

Let me make a general summary here that good governance from a biblical perspective is only possible in the legislature when representation, law-making, public education, supervision of the executive and constitutional and appointive functions of the legislative system are guided by God's grace. This will permit the legislature act as a role model for others in embracing divine grace as the basis of its performance.

But despite the presence of divine grace within and outside the legislative branch of the government, we cannot speak of truly good governance in the legislature unless all the legislative functions are completely submerged in mercy, the third element of divine love.

Mercy

"Be merciful, just as your Father is merciful" (Lk. 6:36). This command by Jesus Himself to us is evidence of the importance of divine mercy. As already established, the legislature ought to carry out its functions in the light of God's mercy for good governance to exist in the legislative branch of government. In the next section, I intend to explore the importance of good governance in the representation, law-making, public education, supervision of the executive and constitutional and appointive functions in the light of God's mercy.

Importance of Mercy in Representation

God's mercy is one of the important fabrics that bind perfectly the electorates and their representative in the process of the legislative representation. This is because mercy enables the two parties to see and address each other's mistakes lovingly. Also, it helps the representative to present the general interests of his constituency in the national forum in a satisfactory and unselfish manner.

But this is not the case sometimes. For example, when the representative lacks God's mercy as part of his ethical code of conduct, he lacks the essence of God's love as well as God himself in his life. This means that he does not actually love the people he alleges to represent because no one can really lead those he does not love. Conversely, people cannot comfortably follow a person who does not love them.

In a nutshell, the merciless representative puts his personal interests above the ones of his constituents. Such a member of parliament is not the voice of the voiceless. So the issues facing his electorates are not known to the government because they are not presented in the national assembly. As a result, voters lose faith in him and in the legislature as well as in the entire government.

But who is really to have the first share of blame in this merciless and corrupt political game? Of course, you know the answer. My aim here is not to apportion blame so as to make people feel guilty. Yet if I were to blame anyone, it would be the electorates because they are the ones who supply our legislatures with necessary manpower. For example, if they show indifference during the time of election, those elected will also portray the same indifference in their execution of important legislative functions like the representation.

What honest contributions do you truly expect from a merciless member of the parliament when issues related to disadvantaged and needy members of the public are tabled for discussion? To tell nothing but the truth, legislature is neither a political trashcan nor an oasis of riches into which unwanted people, social outcasts and poverty-driven people are dumped. On the contrary, it is the noble chamber where important people go to safeguard the national image and sovereignty and people's aspirations. Important things are handled by important people, and that is why men and women working in the national legislative house deserve to be called honourable members. We should sincerely honour some of our people by what they say, do or even think so that when we send them to represent us in our legislative body, others will not fear to call them honourable members.

In as much as their presentation is the process whereby the parliamentarians represent the specific interests of their respective electorates in the parliament, it should be done in the clear light of God's mercy. This is because people, especially the poor, widows and orphans plus other disadvantaged groups, badly need leaders who show mercy to them and present their aspirations humanely and fairly before the national assembly.

In order to execute this noble task mercifully, the Lord expects all the legislative representatives to adopt His divine mercy as the recognisable benchmark of their ethical behaviour. Divine mercy should reflect their tender-heartedness, loving compassion for their people. Such merciful representation is what all legislatures yearn for, for the whole world has voiceless people who need leaders to stand for their rights at national and international level.

Good governance is, therefore, possible in the representation only when the representatives carry out this vital role of the legislature in the light of God's mercy. In the case of representation, it is achievable only when divine mercy becomes the solid foundation upon which the legislature bases its general operations.

Nonetheless, for good governance to be fully realized in the legislature, law-making process should also be carried out in the light of God's mercy.

Importance of Mercy in Law Making

"He has shown you, O man, what is good. And what does the Lord require of you? To act justly and to love mercy and to walk humbly with your God" (Micah 6:8). These famous words by Prophet Micah are a summary of what God requires of His people: to act justly, to show others mercy and to be humble in their relationship with Him. But do our legislators live out this requirement of the Lord? Do they act justly, love mercy and walk humbly with Him and with their fellow human beings as they discharge their noble task of law-making?

Some of the national laws that are enacted in the legislature are totally devoid of divine mercy and do not take into account the interests of the needy masses. Laws should actually be prompted by the desire to show people mercy because the Lord desires that the legislature be a channel for showing mercy. Laws that are not merciful are repressive and humiliating to the people both in the eyes of man and God. For example, majority of the national laws that we frequently see and hear are made in a way that they do not consider the aspirations of the weak, the poor and other disadvantaged members of society. They also disregard the protection and improvement of the ecosystem, and that is why some rare natural species are on the verge of extinction.

As with many other national problems, I see the solution to this one in those who vote in parliamentarians. The way in which electorates choose their legislative representatives is what determines the moral goodness or badness of the legislature. When they choose good people, they get a good legislature. But if they choose bad people, they opt for bad legislature because legislature is nothing more than just the men and women who occupy it.

Hence, if we want our national legislatures to produce state statutes that are bathed thoroughly with the divine mercy, we must choose men and women who base their individual behaviours and social and business friendships on the solid rock of God's mercy.

Why do you expect merciless legislators to produce merciful laws? Sow maize and you won't reap sorghum grains; sow bitter lemon and you won't reap sweet potato. Be sure to reap only what you plant. Parliaments are morally good if their legislators are ethically sound.

The Lord wants the legislators to embrace his divine mercy as the solid mark of their moral values. While they deliberate on some vital legal issues with an eventual aim of enacting them as the state statutes, the legislators must view them through the brightest light of God's mercy by showing their mercy as their tender-heartedness, loving compassion for the people who will in the end be affected by such laws. The laws must reflect human face because they are meant to govern and safeguard human beings.

In concluding this discussion, let me remind the reader that good governance in the law-making process is only possible when all lawmakers have taken God's mercy to be the hallmark of their moral values. This would turn the whole legislative system into an oasis of the divine mercy. This will be evident from the fact that the entire public will be happy with the interpretation and application of the enacted laws. Needless to say, we seriously need merciful legislators who will make laws which when applied will reflect mercy.

But for us to realise truly good governance through a legislature that is guided by God's mercy in doing its work, it is also important for the legislature to carry out its public education role in the light of God's mercy.

Importance of Mercy in Public Education

There are many examples in this world of how legislators who are devoid of the spirit of divine mercy tend not to have mercy towards each other, much less towards other members of the public. They have a spirit that makes them to debate useful national issues in the legislature callously. For instance, they demonstrate indifference when it comes to the pressing needs of the weak and the oppressed, the poor and other disadvantaged and marginalised citizens. But this indifference is most evident when it comes to matters pertaining to the welfare of subhuman creatures living within the national boundaries. This makes the public lose interest in viewing their debates on TV screens, radio sets and in the print media. That way, the legislature fails in its role of public education.

Important national issues demand the administration of men and women who base their ethical code of conduct and social and business relationships on the solid base of God's mercy. But for the national legislature to get this type of personnel, it remains the sole task of the national constituencies. For their national mandate is to choose among themselves merciful people as their legislative representatives. Their mercy will make them capable of discharging the noble function of public education in the right way for the goodness of the whole nation.

For the legislature to carry out public education role in the light of God's mercy, first and foremost, the legislators must adopt God's mercy as the concrete standard of their ethical temperament. They must mercifully behave among themselves. This spirit of the divine mercy will definitely deter them from humiliating one another and assassinating each other's character in the eyes of the general public as they debate and deliberate upon some national issues in the parliament. When they behave mercifully, their divine mercy will automatically permeate the whole legislative system, making it conducive environment for the radiation of God's mercy to other parts of the government.

As a matter of truth, the parliamentarians must discuss all the legislative matters in the light of God's mercy by showing their tenderness of heart towards those involved in such debates. Such discussions should not spring from an ill intention that is meant to smear others' characters with lies and other dirty words in the eyes of the general public and God. This is because this act will not equate with the essence of good governance but with bad governance.

Good governance is only possible in the public education when the legislature discusses all its vital, social and political matters mercifully in the light of God's mercy. If men and women working in the legislature are characterized by divine mercy towards the needy, they could automatically be role models in public education. As a result, good governance will thrive in the legislature.

Nevertheless, if the supervision of the executive is not also guided by the spirit of God's mercy, we cannot truly talk of good governance in the legislature. The primary focus of the following section is to examine the circumstances under which good governance can be demonstrated in the supervision of the executive by the legislature.

Importance of Mercy in Supervision of Executive

In most cases, legislators exercise this vital parliamentary task, not to maintain proper checks and balances and identify and address any malpractices and to ensure better systems in the executive but to name and condemn the culprits and embarrass them in the eyes of the general public. And this is not unexpected because people who are not merciful like to see others crying and writhing in pain and shame. When this crucial task is carried out in the spirit of cruelty, it makes those working in the executive to be more aggressive and defensive. So they hit back harshly against their unfriendly monitors by protecting themselves from what they see as a direct threat to their survival.

This unfriendly approach from the side of the legislature normally creates unhealthy tension between the members of the legislature and those of the executive. And when the two parties are not collaborative and friendly enough, the whole government subsequently becomes very unstable. However, when the legislature mercifully executes its supervisory function on the executive, the latter responds mercifully towards the former.

To totally allay any possible doubt and query in the minds and hearts of my readers, the divine mercy that I am talking about is the one that will enable the legislature to continuously supervise the activities of the executive. It will help it point out any mistakes, bring the wrongdoers to the books of loving justice, rebuke and correct them in love. But it will avoid all sorts of unmerciful behaviour on the part of the legislative members in the whole process.

Attitude of condemnation and unkindness from the legislators towards the executive should be discouraged, for it is contrary to the divine spirit of mercy. It is good for us to know that the Bible does not encourage any types of licentiousness or immorality, for Paul declares: "All Scripture is God-breathed and is useful for teaching, rebuking, correcting and training in righteousness, so that the man of God may be thoroughly equipped for every good work" (2 Tim. 3:16-17).

Therefore, in order to avoid this biased surveillance of the legislature over the affairs of the executive, God highly requires members of the legislature to cherish the divine mercy as the viable cornerstone of their ethical values. It is their tenderness of heart towards the needy that enables them to supervise the work of the executive in the light of God's mercy. The divine mercy of the legislators will saturate the entire legislature. And this will make it a vibrant spring where the whole government draws the essence of good governance for the general welfare of human beings.

As established above, in order for us to speak of good governance in the supervision of the executive, we must staff our national legislatures with people who base their personal behaviour and social and business relations on God's mercy. These men and women should uphold God's mercy as a solid mark of their conduct. Divine mercy ought to engulf the entire legislature and makes it a favourable ground for goodness to thrive.

But in order for us to experience truly good governance within and beyond the legislature, both the constitutional and appointive functions of the legislature must also be carried out in the light of God's mercy.

Importance of Mercy in Constitutional and Appointive Functions

These last functions of the legislature are very important, but when they are abused, the effect to the nation is disastrous. For instance, when the parliamentarians cruelly initiate additions and amendments to the constitution or fully participate in such changes so as to punish their enemies, the effect to the nation is certainly catastrophic. This is because those who feel that their survival is threatened by such changes will plan for counter measures on the decision of the parliamentarians.

This unfriendly situation normally creates a sort of vicious cycle of hatred among members of the public. Likewise, due to their ill motives rather than national interest, when members of the legislature unmercifully approve or reject the appointment of or impeach certain government officials, the consequences will be detrimental, for such unhealthy legislative decisions will in the end create some abhorrence among those involved. This is why we often see and hear some personal and collective wrangling between the legislature and the executive organ. And who really wants such a very unfavourable situation? Only Satan and those who are fully possessed by him are the ones who like such bad relationships. We mostly see and hear these occurrences in our today's corrupt world. As you see, the moment parliamentarians stop to behave ethically, these important legislative roles lose their real meanings and become a selfish avenue for non-ethical gains.

First and foremost, the national electorates are tasked with inalienable role to choose and send to parliament those people who are full of God's mercy and other acceptable moral values. Such honourable members will change for the good their working environment and bring about the essence of good governance in and outside the legislative houses. Under their merciful leadership, the legislative constitutional and appointive functions can be fully implemented and realised. National issues, specifically the fragile ones, need the absolute care and handling of the merciful gentlemen and gentle ladies.

As a result, in order to see some justice done in the legislature in terms of constitutional and appointive functions, God desires that all men and women serving in the legislature must wholeheartedly embrace the divine mercy as a recognisable mark of their moral character. With their divine mercy, the parliamentarians will easily saturate the whole legislature with God's mercy and make it conducive for the discharging of its activities in the light of God's mercy. In the end, this favourable situation can make it easy for us to speak of good governance in and outside the legislature. We need legislative members who have the essence of God's mercy at heart as they deal with their fellow human beings.

To conclude this discussion of good governance in the legislature, we have established that good governance is only possible when its roles of representation, law-making, public education, supervision of the executive and constitutional and appointive functions are guided by God's mercy.

Yet truly good governance in the legislature will still not have been realized if the above legislative functions are not guided by godly persistence, the last element of divine love.

Persistence

Since legislative issues affect both human beings and subhuman creatures, legislative functions should be guided by godly persistence. This is because legislatures that rush and make laws that are not well-thought-out destroy the lives of people and of other living things. The result is a nation that is equally careless and hence, missing valuable things along the narrow and slow path of life and progress.

In this section, I wish to explore good governance in the legislature in the light of God's persistence so far as the legislature's roles—representation, law-making, public education, supervision of the executive, constitutional and appointive functions—are concerned. To do so, I wish to start by exploring how God's persistence can act as a good vehicle that will smoothly deliver good governance in the representation role of the legislature.

Importance of Persistence in Representation

To begin with, it is critical for us to understand that representation is not an easy job, especially when both the constituents and their representative lack the spirit of persistence in their lives. First, as human beings with Adamic nature, the representatives are sometimes distracted by other issues, including their own personal interests, to the extent that they fail to fulfil their promises by not advocating for the rights of their voters in the parliament. In such cases, the voters have the right to complain against them for the sake of their constituencies as well as for their personal relationships. The issue that follows critically needs the essence of divine persistence in their lives so as to enable them see the whole issue in the light of God's love. Second, though the representatives may follow through with their promises by duly presenting their issues in parliament, these issues may not be acted upon immediately. And if the constituents lack divine persistence, they may get weary and lose confidence in good representatives, even questioning their loyalty. Unfortunately, the representatives will impatiently, though logically, respond by throwing their hands in the air and discount on their loyalty to them in turn. In this case, God's persistence is the only strong ligament that can connect the two parties – the constituents and the representatives. This is a normal occurrence in our world today.

To honestly address this constituent-representative's non-persistent problem, first, it is the imperative role of the electorates to choose people who have good moral quality, especially in the area of the divine persistence, to be their representatives in the national legislature. These persistent people will serve them well as they serve the interests of the entire nation. They are types of people who do not easily throw their impatient hands in the air when they are constantly blamed by others. Second, it is also the duty of the same electorates to learn the same spirit of the divine persistence so that they can persevere with their legislative representatives in the course of their presentation. Quick fix things don't normally endure under the sun. So the vital legislative function of representation requires the spirit of God's persistence both on the side of the constituents and representatives if they want to see it done well.

While representing their people before the legislative assembly, legislators should imitate the leadership of Moses of the Bible by being patient under trying circumstances. For instance, though the rebellious Israelites rejected Moses' leadership, he did not abandon them but persistently led them towards the Promised Land. God wants all the parliamentarians to adopt His divine persistence as a permanent trademark of their moral character and yardstick by which they are to measure their daily activities. If they are patient with their voters, the voters will also bear with them in spite of their shortcomings. Such a favourable, friendly circumstance will enhance the presence of good governance in the legislative representation.

I end here by saying that good governance is only possible in the representation function of the legislature when the parliamentarians fully embrace God's persistence as a recognisable mark of their ethical norms and represent the interests of their constituents in the light of God's persistence, irrespective of whether their electorates have similar forbearance or not. Nevertheless, for the whole legislative system to swim in the ocean of good governance in the light of the divine persistence, the law-making process should also be based on God's persistence.

Importance of Persistence in Law Making

Law-making process is a painstaking affair because all situations must be considered and addressed to seal loopholes. In the case of our infant nation of South Sudan as I write, national legislators have been busy drafting, discussing and debating over some vital documents since year 2005 with the hope of enacting them as statutes. Laws that are rashly made make people regret in the end. That is why we hear in different parts of the world some needs for constitutional amendments or reviews so as to remove some clauses and insert new ones in the constitutions.

The primary cause of such half-baked laws is lack of the spirit of divine persistence in the lives of some members of the legislative assembly. The second factor for their shallowness is the lack of the same godly persistence in the lives of the executive members of the government as well as other members of the general public who normally don't give sufficient time to the legislators to do their work of law-making in a satisfactory manner. Although they know the danger of half-baked laws, they lack moral resilience to slow down their intense urge for new constitution.

In order to see our national legislative chambers carrying out successfully this important task of law-making, at least three steps must be taken seriously. First, all the national constituents should exercise maximum and sincere vigilance when they choose their representatives so as to send to parliament men and women of high moral values and who embrace the virtue of God's persistence. These persistent honourable members will deal with their daily national issues in a patient way. Second, the executive and judiciary organs as well as other members of the general public must bear high level of moral tolerance as they relate to and deal with their national legislatures so as to give them amble time to carry on their work, particularly the function of the law-making for the goodness of the whole nation. Third, due to the importance of the legislative matters, especially law-making process, the legislators must persistently execute their work in spite of the impatience of the other members of the public, including the executive and judiciary. This is their national role, and so they have the absolute right to refuse any sort of external pressures which may force them labour quickly, compromise quality and produce very poor product for the badness of the entire nation.

Only when the parliamentarians carry out the law-making process in the very clear light of God's persistence, can we correctly speak of good governance in the legislature. Law-making process demands patience on the part of the lawmakers and other national citizens. Therefore, in order to carry out good law-making process, God expects the legislators to embrace divine persistence as the benchmark for their moral values and the standard by which to execute their work.

In conclusion, good governance is only attainable in the law-making exercise if all lawmakers embrace divine persistence as the trademark of their ethical values and yardstick by which they evaluate their law-making process. Nevertheless, in order for us to achieve truly good governance in the legislative system, public education should also be guided by divine persistence.

Importance of Persistence in Public Education

We live in the age of information technology where change takes place upon change. To keep up with the many changes that are taking place in a short time, even in parliament, issues are discussed and debated in a rush such that some illiterate and slow learners of the public are abandoned in the realm of ignorance. But the situation is made worse when crucial national issues affecting people in some of the remotest parts of the world like newly born Republic of South Sudan where the level of illiteracy is very low are handled by impatient men and women. Of course, people must strive to keep up with the changes in information technology if they are to benefit from it, but we may need to make concessions if we are to carry our people along. Certainly, this is a sacrifice worth making.

If we want to realise fruitful execution of the national public education in our legislative houses, electorates must choose and send men and women who clothe themselves with God's persistence. This spirit of persistence will enable them debate and deliberate on vital national matters persistently in order to keep the general public informed. It is equally required of the general public to constantly change their worldviews in line with the speed of the technological development. Modern education is primarily important in this domain. Above all, the legislators must be persistent like lower primary school teachers when they tackle parliamentary issues in the eyes and the ears of the public. For it is their national obligation to educate all members of the public about issues that affect their lives and the whole nation.

Based on the above explanation, the legislators are expected to persistently carry out their general debates and deliberations in the light of God's persistence. This is simply because when social and political issues are debated patiently and addressed amicably in the light of the divine persistence in the parliament, the general public will get proper public education. This in turn teaches them of how to persistently deal with each other as well as with their legislative representatives in the very light of the divine persistence.

We should know that good governance is only possible in the public education if all members of the legislative assembly embrace firmly divine persistence as the trademark of their moral values and the only lenses through which to view and address vital, social and political matters for the general good of the entire nation.

But for good governance to thrive in the legislature, it is imperative for the legislative supervision of the executive to be done also in the same light of God's persistence.

Importance of Persistence in Supervision of Executive

Supervision of the executive requires absolute care, keenness, sincerity of heart, persistence and objectivity on the part of members of parliament. On the other hand, it calls for openness, patience and honest cooperation on the part of the executive. Without fulfilling those conditions, it will not achieve its noble objective.

Most of the time, members of parliament carry out the legislature's supervisory function with ulterior motive. For example, they could do the work primarily to get hold of the alleged or known wrongdoers so as to warn and punish them seriously. Also, the legislators often have no time for thorough investigation before acting on the matter. But they ought to take time to look into the books of the executive organ as well as the personal and collective business conduct under which mistakes were done.

Generally, the main aim of the supervision tends not to see the best ways of correcting and improving on the executive systems. It rather appears to deal, as mentioned above, impatiently with the related people by serving some with stern warning letters, dismissing others and bringing in new faces into the systems. But the moment the executive detects the legislators' ulterior motives, they immediately withdraw their patience, openness and honest cooperation and declines to work with them harmoniously. This unhealthy trend of the supervision may lead to strife between the two parties as is the case now in some nations.

In order to find better solution to this national issue, these procedures must be followed: first, all the national constituencies are to choose men and women who have high moral norms, especially God's persistence, in their personal behaviours and send them as their representatives to the national legislative assemblies. These are the right people who can persistently carry out the supervision of the executive organ. Also, on the part of the executive branch of the government, high level of the divine persistence is needed. Without this, the executive officials will simply run out of patience and refuse to cooperate with the legislature.

In order for the legislature to play a genuine surveillance role over the vital affairs of the executive, all the legislators should wear the mantle of divine persistence as a clear mark of their moral guidance and transparent eyeglasses through which they are to oversee the national tasks of the executive. In fact, for anyone to carry out an unbiased surveillance over anything, patience should be a prerequisite. So for the legislature to work as acceptable watchdog over the affairs of the executive, it must embrace God's persistence as the recognisable benchmark by which it is to measure its surveillance. Certainly, active dogs are vigilant and patiently watchful, but the persistent legislature should not deal with the executive like a ruthless watchdog.

In ending this section, it is clear that for good governance to flourish in the supervision of the executive, the legislators should fully embrace divine persistence as the emblem of their moral values and the proper yardstick to guide their supervision of the executive. Nonetheless, we cannot comfortably speak of the availability of truly good governance in the legislature if constitutional and appointive functions are not discharged with godly persistence.

Importance of Persistence in the Constitutional and Appointive Functions

When these important functions of the legislature are not carried out properly and with persistence, conflicts between the members of the legislative assembly and members of the general public, especially members of the executive, may occur. One of the common occurrences in our legislatures nowadays is how the legislators hurriedly make amendments (or participate in making changes) to the national constitutions with the motive of protecting their shallow interests. And they do that without caring whether such fast tracked changes in the constitution will have positive effect in the lives of their people. These impatient legislators can also approve or reject some national appointments of key government officials, not necessarily for the welfare of the country but just to meet their narrow aims. They can also carry out unhealthy impeachments of key civil servants in an effort to serve their interests. On the whole, the legislators seem not to have enough time to critically and honestly think through national issues before they take decisions. Very often, critical decisions are hastily made with little regard to their consequences. What kind of governance can be expected from such impatient legislators?

Now in order to have truly good governance in the constitutional and appointive functions of the legislature that is guided by God's persistence, all men and women working in the legislature should adopt divine persistence as the mark of their moral integrity and as a vital cornerstone upon which to base their legislative policies and procedures. Hence, any additions or amendments to the constitution or participation in such changes as well as the approval or rejection of the appointment of key public officers by the legislators should be based on God's persistence. But this cannot happen unless all the national electorates elect people with a high level of godly persistence in their lives and send them to the legislative assembly as their representatives.

Good governance in the constitutional and appointive functions is only possible when all men and women operating in the legislative system firmly embrace divine persistence as the primary benchmark of their moral values and recognisable standard with which they are to measure their daily activities. We badly need patient legislators to patiently carry out their constitutional and appointive functions for the common good of their electorates. Our world seriously needs parliamentarians who are known for forbearance as they deal with those who elected them.

In summary, good governance is only possible in the legislature when representation, law-making, public education, supervision of the executive and constitutional and appointive functions of the legislature are exercised in the light of God's persistence. Also, in order for us to realise good governance and sound ethical values in our national assemblies in the light of God's love, all legislators must base their moral character and business operations on the four dimensions of love: benevolence, grace, mercy and persistence.

Summary

Like the executive branch of government, the legislature cannot experience the essence of good governance and cherished moral values until all its functions—representation, law-making, public education, supervision of the executive, constitutional and appointive—are totally submerged to and guided by the three moral qualities: moral purity, integrity and love. This is to say that unless all the parliamentarians and other workers in the legislature embrace unquestionable moral purity, integrity and divine love, the legislature will continue to be known for moral decay, manifesting it through obvious and hidden forms of corruption and other devilish lifestyles. But for good governance to abound in and outside the legislature, the conduct of parliamentarians must securely and firmly rest on the three cornerstones, which are moral purity, integrity and love.

But for truly good governance in the entire government to exist, judiciary, the third of the three key government organs, must also embrace all the above three elements of moral quality as the firm and reliable pillars of its moral values and ethical practices. This is the subject of the last part of the book.

PART THREE – JUDICIARY
The Importance of Good Governance in the Judiciary

CHAPTER 7
Moral Purity in the Judiciary

CHAPTER 8
Integrity in the Judiciary

CHAPTER 9
Love in the Judiciary

Introduction

Judiciary
It consists of judges and courts

The judiciary is responsible for interpreting the constitution and laws and applying their interpretations to legal disputes brought before the courts. In other words, the judiciary applies the relevant laws, reviews the decisions of the executive branch and evaluates the laws enacted by the government. It is norrmally led by the Attorney General.

To show the importance that God attaches to justice, He commands the judges as follows:

> Do not pervert justice or show partiality. Do not accept a bribe, for a bribe blinds the eyes of the wise and twists the words of the righteous. Follow justice and justice alone, so that you may live and possess the Land your God is giving you (Deut. 16:19-20).

If the judiciary follows justice and justice alone, shunning any sort of bribery in discharging its duties, the spirit of good governance will become evident in all courts of law. All the citizens, whether rich or poor, young or old, male or female, national or alien, will view the law as their personal and corporate protector. That time, there will be no talks of human rights violations or crime against humanity. Since the judiciary is expected to act as a fair arbiter between the executive and legislature in matters pertaining to national laws, a fair judiciary will, accordingly, harmonize the relationship between the executive and the legislature. As a result, a harmonious relationship and proper coordination of work between the three arms of the government, security, political stability, economic prosperity, sound international relations, and other social and cultural benefits will automatically ensue. Then the nation will grow from strength to strength towards its vision. This is a condition under which no one, including the president or Attorney General or the Speaker of the National Assembly, is above the law. The character and conduct of people working within the judicial system is guided by sound moral values, and when things are carried out in such a dignified manner, good governance is realized.

But if judiciary does not "Let justice roll on like a river, and righteousness like a never-falling stream" (Amos 5:24), its work of dispensing justice will be marred by bribery and other vices. The result will be confusion in the judiciary because the advocates of justice will start fighting with the enemies of justice. And of course, 'a house divided against itself cannot stand'. The moment the judicial system misinterprets and misapplies the constitution and the laws that are based on it and nullifies the decisions of the executive branch with ulterior motives—in short, twists the arm of the law to achieve its selfish goal—both the executive and legislature will cease to operate in harmony. This means that the separation of powers and a harmonious working relationship between the three organs of the government will cease to exist. This will lead to anarchy and lawlessness in the government and the state at large. Under such circumstances, the weak and the poor will be exploited by the strong and rich. The rights of foreigners will be violated at will by the uncaring, inhumane nationals. Human rights violation, crimes against humanity, and all other sorts of ills will mushroom uncontrollably. Insecurity, political instability, and economic problems will become common in the nation. Citizens will begin to seek safe haven across their national borders where there is guaranteed food, shelter, protection, etc. Rumors of coup d'état will start going rounds, making the government in power nervous. If this condition continues longer, the nation will eventually earn the unfortunate title of 'failed state', necessitating external intervention to put it back on its feet. This state of affairs is now common in the Arab World and Africa.

Good governance in the judiciary is possible if all legal staff intentionally embrace the right moral values and yield their activities to be guided by them. This part of the book explores the way in which good governance can be realized in the judicial system of the government through the influence of the three aspects of moral qualities—moral purity, integrity and love. Chapter 7 will explore the importance of adopting all the three ingredients of moral purity (holiness, righteousness and justice) in the judiciary as a sound foundation of good governance. In Chapter 8, I look at how the proper upholding of all three elements of integrity (genuineness, veracity and faithfulness) can influence the presence of good governance in the judicial system. Chapter 9 will show the effect on good governance in the legal system when all the judicial personnel base their personal behaviour, their relationships and national duties on all four elements of genuine love (benevolence, grace, mercy and persistence).

Chapter 7
Moral Purity in the Judiciary

Compromised Judiciary

The judiciary is responsible for interpreting the Constitution and the various laws and applying them to resolve disputes brought before the courts. But even in the judiciary, there is no shortage of negative role models. Legal institutions under the purview of the judiciary have been known for moral decay, with those manning them allowing themselves to be compromised through corruption. The upshot is the rich and powerful using their influence to subjugate the poor. People's rights, whether local or alien, are violated at will, resulting in insecurity, political instability, and economic collapse as investors leave for more stable environments. Citizens may also flee and seek safety across national borders. If the condition persists, the nation earns the unfortunate title of 'failed state', necessitating external intervention as the international community seeks ways to put it back on its feet. This state of affairs is now common in the Arab world and in Africa.

To remedy the situation, those in the judiciary should learn to redefine their relationship with money and embrace godly principles that will enable them do their work of dispensing justice honourably. Activities, even those that have to do with making money, should never be regarded as more important than one's nation.

Importance of Moral Purity in the Judiciary

Judiciary envelops courts of law, judgement or judges. Collectively, it means judges of a state. It is the branch of the central authority in any given state, and it is mandated with judicature or the administration of justice. As already mentioned, it comprises the entire system of courts and judges.

Courts protect property rights, the rights of the people and the rights of the state. It is their duty to interpret and enforce national statutes. They are responsible for handling disputes between other arms of the government, between them and the Non-governmental Organizations (NGOs) as well as between individuals and institutions. But the way the judiciary functions depends largely on the nation's political system—military, parliamentary democracy, presidential democracy, etc.

In Africa, the structure of the judiciary and a nation's laws tend to borrow heavily from the laws of the former colonial masters. In Anglophone countries, the judiciary is guided by customary or indigenous Africa law, religious law and English law, whereas the judiciary in Francophone countries employs customary law, religious law and French laws.

The public persecutor and the police are the major law enforcement agencies. Unfortunately, in many cases, especially in Africa, the police force is misused by the executive to quell justified demonstrations as well as hunt down political opponents against the will of the judiciary. Also, judges often face some unnecessary political interference in the course of their work. And the reason the judiciary lacks independence is because judges are appointed and removed from office at will by the executive. The security of tenure that the judges enjoy always gives the public the impression that they are above the manipulation of politicians, but this is not the case because they are sometimes victimised over certain legal decisions.

In the remaining part of the book, let us see how good governance can be actualized through an independent judicial system that has all the ten divine aspects of God's moral purity, integrity and love.

> If we claim to be without sin, we deceive ourselves and the truth is not in us. If we confess our sins, he is faithful and just and will forgive us our sins and purify us from all unrighteousness. If we claim we have not sinned, we make him out to be a liar and his word has no place in our lives (1 Jn. 1:8-10).

Based on the above biblical truth, do we sin daily by our words, deeds and thoughts? And if we do, are we willing to admit and confess and beseech God to forgive us of our sins and purify us from all unrighteousness? If you answer in the affirmative, especially if you are judge in the court of law, the Holy God will purify you from all unrighteousness (all types of moral impurity, including, of course, all forms of corruption) and give you a fresh start.

This is the only way by which we can regain our lost moral purity. There are no shortcuts. Needless to say, coercing people cannot make them morally pure. Crafting and enacting stern national laws to govern people's moral behaviour will intimidate and influence them to behave cowardly, suspiciously and deceivingly but not make them pure. Forcing people to behave in a certain way against their will is just like giving a sponge an abnormal shape through pressing, only to release your grip and it immediately goes back to its normal shape.

I believe the best way for a person to regain his moral purity is for him to humbly acknowledge his sins, go back and bow before the throne of God and sincerely pray, repenting and asking for His forgiveness and receiving it in faith. Henceforth, he should then continually walk side by side with God, yielding to Him to live and work through you.

In this section, we will examine the influence on good governance in the judiciary of all the elements of moral purity, that is, holiness, righteousness and justice. Let us begin by looking at how good governance in the judiciary can be brought about by executing all judicial activities in the light of God's holiness.

Holiness

From the background that I have given on the judiciary, it is clear that national statutes are sacred, as they affect the lives of national citizens, their collective and personal possessions as well as the national sovereignty. Since people are religious beings, the laws also protect the freedom of worship. In the case of South Sudan, the religions include Islam, Christianity and Africa Traditional Religion (ATR), among others.

The statutes should be interpreted and applied justly as God requires. Unfortunately, this is not usually the case. For example, in some parts of the globe, important national laws are mishandled by men and women who have no fear of God in their lives. All they have is inflated ego arising from their professional training. Yet these judges are totally devoid of the divine philosophy of human life. And even if they are aware of it, they don't consider it when passing judgment, especially when condemning people to death over minor offences that do not even deserve what is termed as "life sentence" in the developed countries. Their legal knowledge and pride have badly seared their conscience to the extent that they have lost the sense of humanity.

Other times, important matters that touch on the national image and sovereignty are handled by the same judges without seriousness and due respect. This lack of seriousness and respect in the interpretation and application of the national statutes by unholy judges often lead to individual, societal, national and international unrests.

It is the primary duty of both the executive and the legislature to exercise due care when appointing senior judges, like Attorney General and Chief Justice. These should be people who bear moral purity, especially holiness as their unique attire. When such key appointments are based purely on educational qualifications, both the nation and its citizens suffer tremendously from callous interpretation and application of the law. Besides knowledge of the law, those who want to be judges should also demonstrate a blend of moral excellence and personal piety. Holy matters should be handled by holy people.

After a discourse on doctrine, reminding us that God is our Father and we as His sons and daughters in 2 Cor. 6:18, Apostle Paul then tells the believers, "Since we have these promises, dear friends, let us purify ourselves from everything that contaminates body and spirit, perfecting holiness out of reverence for God" (2 Cor. 7:1). In order to perfect holiness through reverence for God and because of their being created in the image and likeness of God, our court judges should purify themselves and their judicial system from everything, including any kind of moral corruption which contaminates body and spirit, of course. This will help them, as they will be able to honourably discharge their national obligations, thereby ushering in the spirit of good governance, not only in the judiciary but in the entire nation as well.

Furthermore, it is good for us to understand that for men and women working in the judiciary to excel in their national tasks as God's appointees, they must consecrate themselves, becoming holy, just as God is holy. They should be morally pure and not defile themselves with any sort of corruption. Because the whole ethical code flows from the holiness of God, officers in the judiciary should embrace God's perfection as the standard of their moral character. If they are not holy, how will they judge others on the basis of God's holiness? You cannot wash dirty things with dirty water or clean dirty things with dirty objects. Dirty things are washed with clean water. Likewise, for the courts to administer proper justice among ungodly people, judges must, first and foremost, examine their own character in the light of God's holiness. After all, God is the ultimate judge of all things. Hence, it is good for the judges to gauge their own personal character against the holiness of God for the judicial system to be how it ought to be.

If judges, as the law-enforcing agents, adopt God's holiness and internalise its essence to be part of their lives, they will automatically reap God's blessings and divine power to discharge their judicial work for the common good of God's people and also for the glory of God. It is only when holy judges sit in the holy courts and interpret and apply holy laws in the light of God's holiness and impart justice to those in dire need can good governance be said to exist in the judiciary. Apart from their judicial expertise, we badly need holy judges nowadays in our courts to tackle legal issues in the light of God's holiness.

When all judges and their judicial system swim in the lake of God's holiness, sufficient presence of good governance in and outside the judiciary will be realised. But we cannot end here without examining it also in the clear light of the divine righteousness, the second element of moral purity.

Righteousness

In order for us to properly understand how God wants us to craft and apply the law, the following words of the Psalmist reflect the importance of righteous statutes:

> The law of the Lord is perfect, reviving the soul. The statutes of the Lord are trustworthy, making wise the simple. The precepts of the Lord are right, giving joy to the heart. The commands of the Lord are radiant, giving light to the eyes. The fear of the Lord is pure, enduring forever. The ordinances of the Lord are sure and altogether righteous (Ps. 19: 7-9).

When we think of the law, we often think of something that keeps us from having fun. But the Bible says the opposite – God's law makes us wise, brings joy to the heart, gives us insight, warns us, makes us righteous, makes us morally good and rewards us. God's law is a guide and a light to our path, not a hindrance to our hands and feet. It warns us of danger and points us to the way forward for success. It is a guide to us.

Going by the above biblical quotation, the work of the judiciary is to educate the general public about the perfection, trustworthiness and righteousness of the national laws. Its other role is to interpret the statutes to make them a radiant light to the eyes of the public and show them the direction of purity and righteousness.

However, most of the time our national laws are interpreted and applied within and outside the national borders in unrighteous style by the unrighteous men and women in judicial uniforms. That is, they are discharged in a way that the rights of the oppressed, the rights of the poor and the rights of the weak and other disadvantaged citizens are gravely violated. At the same time, the national image and sovereignty as well as the environment are not considered in the process of the interpretation and application. So instead of giving hope to the souls, the laws destroy them; instead of their trustworthiness, they become untrustworthy; instead of giving joy to the heart, they bring grieve; instead of bringing light to the eyes, they bring darkness, and instead of promoting righteousness, they facilitate unrighteousness. How can one expect unrighteous judges to interpret and correctly apply righteous laws?

For the laws to be justly applied, they need righteous men and women to interpret them. God expects all judicial officials to be righteous in their thoughts, words and actions because He puts them where they are so as to judge His people righteously. Their righteousness must indicate that their actions are in line with the laws that they themselves are interpreting and applying. In other words, their actions should be in conformity with what they expect from others and be a true expression of what they require.

But for our judicial systems to be just and respectful, both the executive and the legislature must resist the temptation to compromise their trust and ethical code of conduct while making appointments of senior judicial officials. Judges should be men and women who base their personal behaviour and social and business relationships on the solid rock of God's righteousness. Righteous people have the absolute right and moral integrity to deal with right and sacred issues for the goodness of mankind.

If the judiciary takes divine righteousness as the concrete foundation on which it interprets and applies the national laws on real, social and political issues, good governance in the judiciary and in other organs of the government will be enhanced. In other words, good governance is only possible in the judiciary if all legal issues are carefully addressed in the light of God's righteousness. We do not just want judges who sound educated but also just men and women who manage the judicial system for the general welfare of human beings and also for God's own glory.

But it is also fair for us to see how the practical use of divine justice can usher in the essence of good governance in and outside the judiciary.

Justice

In political systems worldwide, the laws and courts that interpret and apply them appear to favour judicial system itself, the state and its ruling elite. The manner in which both the ruling elite and the state assess their interests shows inconsistency from system to system. But in most instances, judicial systems are devoid of godly justice and that leads others to have the contempt of the courts in the area of legal matters. Also it makes the judicial systems subject to a lot of national criticisms and contempt of the courts.

It is quite incredible to see the actual interpretations and applications of the national statutes in our today's world in direct denial of the rights of the weak, the rights of the poor, the rights of the oppressed and other disadvantaged members of the public in the courts of justice. Where is true justice in our nations if the strong and the rich plus those with strong leadership connections are well served and covered by the same national laws at the very expense of the unfavourable members of the same nation? Where is true justice if the righteous and the innocence are convicted and punished while the wicked and the wrongdoers are set free in our judicial courts? Where is the core of justice in our nations if judicial decisions are greatly influenced by hideous elements of bribery? Impartial laws are never ever imperial laws; otherwise, they are unjust and repressive ordinances in the eyes of God and man. Unjust interpretations and applications of the national statutes in the realm of mankind is the primary cause of some national and international socio-economic and political mayhems and strife.

In order to make the courts of law the actual mirror of divine justice, the Lord expects judges to exercise justice when cases are brought before them. For the holy command reads:

> Appoint judges and officials for each of your tribes in every town the Lord your God is giving you, and they shall judge the people fairly. Do not pervert justice or show partiality. Do not accept a bribe, for a bribe blinds the eyes of the wise and twists the words of the righteous. Follow justice and justice alone, so that you may live and possess the land the Lord your God is giving you (Deut. 16:18-20).

As is clearly seen in the above passage of Scripture, God requires judges and other court officials to judge the people fairly without perverting justice or showing partiality. Neither are they supposed to accept any form of bribe from those seeking justice. Instead, they are to pursue justice and justice alone relentlessly in their judicial ministry. They are to show justice to the afflicted by letting it rolls down like winter snows, for the Bible further says clearly: "… To show partiality in judging is not good: Whoever says to the guilty, 'You are innocent'- peoples will curse him and nations denounce him. But it will go well with those who convict the guilty, and rich blessing will come upon them" (Pr. 24:23-25).

To follow this biblical command in our judicial systems, both the executive organ and the legislature are to critically and analytically examine and weigh the moral ingredients of those who are supposed to preside over our national judiciaries so as to avoid appointing men and women with clear moral defects in their personal behaviours. An obvious element of moral justice is one of the strongest criteria for the appointment or election of courts judges, especially in the choice of the Chief Justice and Attorney General. Otherwise, it will be a direct misapplication of the English term (justice), if a judge does not own this unique moral character. We must practise what we preach.

Good governance is only possible in the judiciary when all judges and other judicial officials adopt God's justice as the foundation upon which to base their personal conduct. Also, good governance is only possible in the judiciary if all its staffs exercise or pursue their legal matters in the light of God's justice. Before expecting others to uphold God's justice, let our judicial personnel take the divine justice as the cornerstone of their individual lives as well as a viable apparatus with which they are to tackle their legal issues for the betterment of man and also for the glory of the Lord.

In recap, allow me to underscore here the fact that good governance is only possible in the judiciary in the light of moral purity, when all the judicial personnel base their individual lives and all their activities on the solid foundation of holiness, righteousness and justice. Nonetheless, truly good governance will still be lacking if the same personnel fail to surrender themselves and their judicial system to all pertinent dimensions of the divine integrity. This is the focus of the following chapter.

Chapter 8
Integrity in the Judiciary

To underscore the importance of the integrity and the significance of the judiciary and their inseparableness, allow me to begin here with the following leadership prayer:

You know how I want people to agree with me and believe in me. It is so easy for me to say what others want to hear instead of what I honestly feel or believe. It is so natural for me to commit before I am positive I can deliver because someone needs something and I want to give it. Oh, God, set your Spirit at the door of my mouth, and guard what I say. Keep me honest and realistic.

Lord, in our markets, image is everything. My own image as the leader is a highly visible part of our organizational image. Very often I am all that people know about the organization, and they read the fine print of what they see in me. If I do not seem genuine to them, they will assume the organization is not genuine either. Protect me from even the slightest fault of acting out of character.

Lord, I am not the leader every moment, but I am myself every moment. Those I lead depend on my integrity. Do not let me ever embarrass them, not as their leader and not as the real me inside the leader role. Make them save in their dependence on me.

Don't let the fame and visibility that go with this leadership role fool me into forgetting the difference between myself and my role. Don't let me make the blunder of needing to be a celebrity. But by your grace, God, I would really love to be a genuine hero. I long to make a great difference in people's lives. I want to walk away someday and know that together we did something special and that we all became better people in the process... God, you are absolutely who you claim to be. Keep me true to myself.[14]

Just as our national leaders upon whose integrity the poor and the rich, the young and the old, the weak and the strong, the male and the female depend, judges need to keep true to themselves so as not to embarrass people but make them feel safe as they depend on them. Judges should be leaders of dependable integrity whose courts are the reliable spring of human rights and life.

In this section, we will examine ways and means by which good governance can be achieved in and outside the judiciary in the light of the divine integrity. The discussion will focus mainly on trying to see how judicial staff can embrace the spirit of genuineness, veracity and faithfulness as the cornerstone of their personal moral values and the basis on which to execute their day-to-day work. Let's start by exploring how good governance in the judiciary can be attained in the light of genuineness.

---

14 Ibid.,Kriegbaum, 86-87.

Genuineness

Nowadays, when people talk about the absence of good governance in government, the judiciary is not exempted. In almost all the nations around the world, people keep complaining about the spreading scourge of corruption in the judicial system. Corruption in the judiciary is a reminder of the manner in which the court officials wrongly interpret and apply the national statutes before God and man.

The fact of the matter is that the long processes through which bills go in the national assembly in the hearing of the public before they become law makes them to be perceived as fair. They are the reliable laws which govern government norms of operations, people's behaviours and their social and business relationships. They also define and protect the sovereignty of the nation in the community of nations. In short, national statutes are specific and realistic.

But the problem comes when they are interpreted and applied by men and women who lack God's genuineness in their moral character. Their lack of realness makes them hide behind the darkest shadow of the law, interpreting and applying the essence of the law wrongly to achieve their ill motives. And when they are confronted for their wrong acts, they try to absolve themselves and put the whole blame on the law. That is why we always hear some judges saying, "It is not I who did it but the law." Poor and un-genuine lawyers seem to take advantage of people's limitation of legal knowledge. And that is where the authenticity and the justness of the national laws come in to support members of the public who appear not to understand their legal rights.

People believe that one of the reasons for the absence of good governance in the judiciary is lack of divine genuineness in the courts and in the personal lives of its officials. This lack (or scarcity) of the divine genuineness within and outside the four corners of the judiciary has, unfortunately, led to the contempt of the judicial systems.

In order to find some possible solutions to this moral and legal problem, it is the primary duty of both the executive organ and the legislature to make sure that those appointed to the higher levels of judiciary must be men and women who are of high moral calibre, specifically in relation to the genuineness of their personal behaviours. Then they will be the ones to instil good moral values in the minds and the hearts of their junior judicial officials. Judges should not be people who behave like chameleons but should be real like the genuine Lord. As a matter of fact, genuine laws need their genuine interpretations and applications from genuine legal experts. Unfortunately, the bodies entrusted with the work of appointing judges sometimes appoint judges, especially the Chief Justice and the Attorney General, not for the benefit of the judiciary and the entire nation but simply to take care of their narrow interests.

Inasmuch as the judiciary is one of the main pillars of the government and the only torchbearer when it comes to interpreting and applying of laws in any nation, God wants all men and women operating in the judicial systems to adopt His divine genuineness as the cornerstone of their moral character. He seriously wants them to be true to themselves, to be true to the national laws, to be true to God and to be true to fellow citizens. Actually, we badly need genuine judges to enforce high integrity among the people through the genuine interpretation and application of the national statutes among the general public for the general welfare of human beings and also for the glory of the Lord.

In concluding the discussion, may I mention in summary that good governance is only possible within and outside the judiciary only when all judges uphold the divine genuineness as the fundamental basis of their own behaviour. Then, based on their own authenticity, these judges are able to genuinely execute all the legal interpretations and the applications of the state statutes in the clear light of God's genuineness within and outside the national boundaries. Our courts badly need genuine judicial personnel to guide and guard the interpretation of genuine laws, respecting no one but itself. However, it is also good for us to see below how veracity, the second dimension of integrity, can influence the presence of good governance in the judiciary.

Veracity

Looking now from the angle of honesty, I feel I can rightfully conclude here that good governance in the judiciary is incomplete without seeing judicial issues as well as the lives of its staff in the light of God's veracity. It is very insignificant for us to speak of good governance in the judiciary if the judicial system is not based on the divine honesty through which it can correctly view legal matters. Also, it is not possible for us to talk about honesty in the judiciary if all the court officials are notably dishonest with themselves, dishonest with God and dishonest with other members of the public. Actually, the mere understanding of complicated legal jargons does not make judge good if he lacks divine moral values, for the wise has this uncompromising advice: "The Lord detests lying lips, but he delights in men who are truthful" (Prov. 12:22).

Our world is inundated with liars, people who can persuasively defend their actions while a critical look at their reasoning reveals untruthfulness. So far as they are concerned, one is free to lie and manufacture some doubtful grains of truth to camouflage those lies in order to win the argument.

This is the way some of the best and most respected diplomats, politicians and lawyers are.

But this sheer dishonesty is totally disgraceful, embarrassing and dehumanising when it is carried out within the four corners of the judicial house. It is not good because the general public thirst for the divine veracity, and the only reliable social institution which is expected to avail it to the people is the Judiciary. The poor, the weak, the oppressed and the marginalised people look up to the judiciary to protect them and help them access their rights. Even the rich and the strong sometimes need honesty in the interpretation and application of the national laws.

In view of the above, what do you expect when national laws are interpreted and applied in and outside the national setting by men and women who are known for their dishonesty? Well, your answer is as good as mine.

If national laws are to be applied in an honest manner in the judiciary for the general good of the masses as well as for the benefit of the whole nation, the presence of honest judges to handle them is very crucial. But this cannot happen unless the executive organ and the legislature play their part by appointing honest judges, like Attorney General and Chief Justice, to preside over the legal affairs of the nation. These have the power and clout to enforce the divine veracity within the judicial systems. Of course, you don't expect justice to abound in the judiciary when laws are interpreted and applied by dishonest men and women.

In order to bring divine honesty within the four corners of the judicial system, all members of the courts must adopt God's veracity wholeheartedly as the primary mark of their moral values. They must truthfully present things as they are. As people dealing with the legal matters, they are also expected to show that what they say can always be trusted. They must be honest in all situations. They are to be trustworthy both in what they formally assert and in what they imply.

Therefore, we can comfortably speak of good governance in the judiciary when divine honesty is one of the strongest pillars upon which the judicial system rests and discharges its duties. Also, we can talk about the presence of good governance in the judiciary without any slight hesitation if all the courts members uphold the divine truthfulness as the firm basis of their individual ethical code of conduct and if they carry out their judicial activities in the light of God's veracity.

We seriously need honest courts, courts that are manned by dependable men and women who interpret and apply the state laws in the light of God's veracity for the benefit of human beings and for the glory of the Lord as well.

But whenever the lives of the judicial officials are not completely based on divine faithfulness, the last element of integrity, we cannot say that real good governance is assured in and beyond the judicial domain. So follow me as I examine below the possibility of having good governance in judiciary in the light of faithfulness.

Faithfulness

It is worth mentioning here that any judicial system that is not based on the divine faithfulness is obviously not qualified to interpret and apply the state statutes within and beyond the national boundaries. Of course, one must, first and foremost, need to be morally sound before he qualifies to make proper judgement on moral issues.

The current trend so far as legal matters are concerned is that many people in the world, especially in the Third World countries, have lost faith in the sincerity and reliability of their national statutes. One of the main reasons is that judicial procedures are made in a way that it is hard, if not impossible, for the common man to have easy access to justice in his own land. For instance, the cost of accessing justice in the courts of law is so high it is beyond the reach of the average citizen. Lengthy judicial procedures in certain nations translate into denial of justice, a waste of vital and meagre resources (time, energy and money in particular). As a case in point, I personally know of a lady in Juba, South Sudan, whose case for a residential property has been in court undecided for more than four years. As I write, this case has taken vast amounts of her personal resources and the matter is still not concluded. As a result, some people have abandoned the pursuit of their rights through the courts of law. Above all, when the laws are handled dishonestly by some known faithless men and women in the courts, people lose faith in the application of their laws.

In order to address the above legal challenges, both the executive and the Legislature should choose men and women who have impeccable good moral values, those who are faithful to themselves, faithful to their own nations and faithful to mankind as a whole to be in charge of their national judiciaries. These faithful judges will transform the judicial systems and thus, make them reliable oasis of justice where all the people, old and young, rich and poor, weak and strong satisfactorily quench their legal thirst.

God expects all men and women working in the judicial system, especially judges, to emulate His divine faithfulness as the principal basis of their moral character so as to have a positive impact on the laws and the courts that interpret and apply them. For instance, all judges should show their faithfulness by proving true by keeping all their promises. As they deal with legal matters, the judges should not commit themselves to carry out any interpretations and applications of the national laws if they know they will not be able to do so. They cannot give some legal backing thoughtlessly. And when they do, they are to remain faithful to them under all circumstances because the words of their judgement have the power to sustain life or end it. Their explicit faithfulness will automatically make the whole judicial structure to operate in the light of God's faithfulness.

Fair interpretation and application of national laws has desirable national and personal consequences. For example, it increases public confidence in the court system and its judges with a returning trust from the judges to the general public. Also, fair interpretation and application of the state laws brings about harmony among members of the public, peace and prosperity to the rest of the nation and God's blessings upon the whole land, especially the judicial system. Also, proper interpretation and application of the national laws results in good governance within and beyond the national boundaries.

Good governance is possible in the Judiciary when the interpretation and application of the national statutes is done by faithful judges, using just law-enforcement agencies. Our world is not interested only in formidable and impressive court buildings in which faithless and merciless judges dwell. The world is looking for humane and faithful courts that house faithful and loyal judges who fear God. They should be faithful in the interpretation and application of the state laws in accordance with God's will because this is what the Lord wants.

As I conclude this section, may I repeat that good governance is possible in the judiciary when all the relevant staff take genuineness, veracity and faithfulness, the three aspects of the divine integrity, as the foundation upon which they base their general judicial policies and operations. And the same faithfulness is to be the basis of their own personal lives and moral values.

But the complete essence of good governance will still be lacking unless we also submerge the entire judicial system in the ocean of divine love, the last component of moral qualities. This is the focus of Chapter Nine.

Chapter 9
Love in the Judiciary

Do judges see their clients as unlovable criminals who deserve nothing more than damnation? Or do they see them as helpless people seeking justice through their trusted loving judges in the courts of law? What is the expected character of a good judge? Must he exude cruelty to discharge justice well, or is it possible to show divine affection towards those before him without compromising the law?

It is good for us to know that in almost all cases, judges in the courts of law look intimidating, inaccessible and vindictive and above human. They instil in the people they are serving unnecessary fear, and are a cause of low self-esteem and feeling of hopelessness. You go to the courts of law and the unfriendly atmosphere there makes you feel like not going there again even when you are not the accused. But are members of the public supposed to fear their own judges, their own brothers and sisters, or are they expected to respect and love them as their protectors? Of course the courts are not supposed to be a place where people go to joke like in the market place; it is the place where wrong doers are dealt with. Nevertheless, the courts of law need a human face as well.

It is common for lawbreakers to feign remorse and helplessness with the hope of being shown mercy from the four corners of the law courts. Hence, in dealing with such, I expect our judges learn from God about whom the Bible says, "For God so loved the world that he gave his one and only Son, that whoever believes in him shall not perish but have eternal life. For God did not send his Son into the world to condemn the world, but to save the world through him" (Jn. 3:16-17).

Who is our spiritual Supreme Judge? And who loves sinners, God's true opponents? Well, the Lord is our loving Supreme Judge and the Lover of sinners (the past and the present ones), including I and you. I believe you do agree with me that our law courts are not there merely to condemn people but to maintain law and order by interpreting and applying lovingly the national statutes among the sons and the daughters of the same nation. Although they impose punishments on the culprits, they are, unless otherwise, not the ones doing it per se but just guiding the law to follow its own course. In fact, when judges administer the law in love among people, they are really fulfilling the essence of the law, protecting and upholding the entire national and individual interests as is clearly spelled out in the book of Romans: "Love does no harm to its neighbour. Therefore love is the fulfilment of the law" (Rom. 13:10).

In this last part of the book, I shall devote my discussion to the ways and means by which some moral excellence can be achieved in and outside the judiciary when all its staff and activities are based on the solid ground of benevolence, grace, mercy and persistence, the four elements of God's love. Let's now see the way benevolence can promote good governance in the judiciary.

Benevolence

The presence of good governance in the judiciary is very important in the life of any national government because as we know, the judiciary consists of a system of courts and officials, for instance judges, who interpret and apply national laws within and beyond the national boundaries. In our current world, people are afraid of their lawyers more than their own national laws. But real national statutes are actually made by the people and for the people. So people love, fear and respect them. But there are many reasons that make people to fear their lawyers than the actual laws they interpret and apply. First and foremost, some people, especially in the Third World, do not thoroughly understand the laws that govern them. So when they come into direct conflict with them, and the law takes its course, the wrongdoer cries foul by blaming the law enforcers, especially the judge. In this case, he does not differentiate the law from its implementer. Second, even when the law is correctly interpreted and applied by a lawyer albeit in an unkind manner, the victim of the law will hate the lawyer more than the law itself. This is simply because when the whole legal process is not guided by divine benevolence, it becomes harsh and unfriendly in the eyes of the convict. But if the law is the one to condemn or to release, then there is no need for the judge being rude, since he is merely implementing the law.

In 2003, Mr. Kon Deng and I embarked on a journey by land from Sioux Fall in South Dakota going to Fargo in North Dakota in USA. Kon was the one driving. As we were on the highway, we could see that the authorized maximum speed was 70 miles per hour. But as the distance we were supposed to cover was long, Kon was frequently tempted to slightly exceed this limit. But as a person who likes to abide by the law, I kept telling him to slow down and maintain the regulated speed. So his driving speed kept going up and down. We continued with the journey, chatting and listening to music by the famous musician, the late Teresa Nyankol Mathiang. As a result, I temporarily neglected my role of keeping an eye on his speed.

Not long after, I realized Kon was no longer involved in the conversation. Glancing at him, I saw him stepped on the brake while peeking at the car mirror. As a first time visitor in the States, I did not immediately understand what was happening. Not to keep me in suspense, my friend Kon softly and sadly told me, "We have been caught for over-speeding. The police car is behind ours." Under such circumstances in most African countries, the driver is likely to stop the car, come out of the vehicle and meet the traffic police by the roadside or anywhere else and discuss the way forward. So I decided to open the door and come out, but Kon, a USA citizen, stopped and told me that the policeman was going to come. So we just waited inside.

Shortly after, a heavily built but humble policeman approached us and said, "Hi sirs, what the rush today!"

"Are we rushing, sir?" Kon asked.

"Yes, 75", he replied.

Indeed, by the time we were caught Kon was driving at 75 miles per hour.

He went on and said, "Can I see your driver's licence, sir?"

Kon got into his pocket, produced the driver's licence and proffering it to him said, "Here, sir."

Then he took it and said, "Wait for me, sirs."

"Alright, sir," we replied.

As all this was going on, my mind was engaged in contrasting the friendly attitude of the law enforcers in the States with the hostile attitude of law enforcers back in Africa when confronted with wrongdoing of the same magnitude. But before I could reach my conclusion, the same policeman returned to us and gave Kon his licence back and a ticket with the following comments: "Sir, you have violated the traffic rule and are therefore fined $85. Please go and pay it into the bank later at your own convenience". Then he said, "Enjoy your journey, sirs." So he went back to his car and we continued on our long journey, not driving recklessly again this time but strictly following the traffic regulations.

My first reaction as we continued with our conversation was to wonder how kind the traffic police were to the members of the public. Kon responded by saying that that is the attitude expected of them by the national law. They have to deal with people in a kind and loving manner, unless one has shown a kind of violent behaviour to them. Yet even if they have to use force, they are to do that with full restraint. Did the law take its due course? How was the attitude of the policeman towards us? Do we see the same humane attitude in our law enforcers in our parts of the African, specifically in the newly born Republic of South Sudan? If not, why and what should be done to change the state of affairs?

The third reason why people fear law enforcers more than the law itself is the way the law is misinterpreted and misapplied by unkind judges in the public. This is a clear violation of judicial ethics. Such judges seek to achieve their own selfish interests through the judiciary by pretending to be serving the national interests and people's aspirations. As a result, people are afraid of them, for they do not see them as their own legal protectors and justice providers but merely as their enemies in judicial garb.

To underscore this point, let me take you back to the lady I mentioned earlier whose justice has been delayed by a court of law in Juba. One time, the judge handling her case harshly rebuked her, even subjecting her to racial slur. During the proceedings, she had tried to respond to the judge's question in the English Language, but the judge had angrily responded to her in Arabic, saying, "Don't talk to me in English. My mother isn't an English woman." Feeling intimidated, this humble, poor lady had apologised and switched to Arabic. The irony is that though this judge speaks and required his clients to speak Arabic, his mother is not an Arab, either. Besides, the Constitution recognizes English as an official language in the Republic of South Sudan.

What do you think would have happened to such an uncouth judge if he did what he did in a nation where judicial ethics are steadfastly upheld? Should the courts of law be the place where those who seek nothing but justice are intimidated, insulted by judicial officials who are supposed to be the protectors and providers of people's rights, letting justice roll on like a mighty river and righteousness like a never-ending stream? (Amos 5:24).

Of course, it is not the entire judicial system in South Sudan that experiences such inhumane, cruel and uncivilised abuse of the courts of law by its officials. The Constitution even provides for an interpreter in the courts where a client doesn't speak either English or Arabic. The uncouth judge in question happens to be one of those who access judicial powers through educational qualifications but lacks the proper morals as a result of which his bad behaviour reflects badly and could negatively affect an otherwise dignified judicial systems and the entire nation as well.

How can we have people-centred, God-fearing and benevolent judges in our national courts systems? In answering this question, both the executive organs and the legislature are mandated to ensure that our judiciary is manned by men and women of high moral values, especially divine benevolence, an important element of God's love. Good moral values will help them saturate the whole judicial systems with moral goodness and make them avenues of good governance. Vital national laws must not be handled by loveless people because they are meant for the betterment of mankind as well as for God's own glory.

In addition, all courts officials should embrace God's benevolence as the yardstick of their ethical values. This essential, divine virtue will make them to kindly and unselfishly interpret and apply the national laws with the ultimate welfare of the general public in mind. Judicial officials should not interpret and apply the state statutes just to meet their own narrow interests and those of the ruling elite. They should work at realizing the general aspirations of the entire public. This is simply because their narrow interests are just but a small part of the public interest, not the other way around.

It is also good for me to point out here that the legislators should not be biased in the interpretation and application of the state laws. That is to say, in their interpretation and application of the state laws, they should not favour some particular people at the expense of others. If anything, laws should be applied to all the citizens without bias, just as God's sun rises to both good and bad people (Matt. 6:26, 28), satisfying the desire of every living thing (Ps. 145:16). Moreover, in applying the laws we should remember that they are just meant for moral correction but not for the humiliation of certain people and destruction of subhuman creatures.

For good governance to abound in the judiciary for the common benefit of mankind and for God's own glory, both the system of the courts and its officials who interpret and apply the national laws must allow themselves to be guided by God's benevolence as the benchmark by which all judicial issues are judged. Court officials should therefore, understand that for their work to succeed, they need to portray great selflessness, an element of divine love, as an aroma that pleases the Lord. Apart from other vital attributes of the judges, we highly require their divine benevolence, for it is very hard, perhaps impossible, to serve others if you don't love them.

Truly speaking, the presence of benevolence in the judiciary system is not sufficient enough to usher in good governance unless the entire judicial system is also brought under the magnifying glasses of grace, the second element of God's love. This is the focus of following section.

Grace

In fact the war is not between the society and those who work in the judiciary. The war is between the national law itself and the people, including judges. People are people, and the law is supposed to be above all the people, including the President. But have you ever seen a judge arrayed in the courts of law? Yes, this keeps on happening because the law is supposed to be a respecter of none other than itself. The law is there to govern the social and business relationships of the people as well as the national sovereignty and the nation's operations.

When the judicial procedures and operations lack God's grace in them, they become oppressive to the members of the public. Graceless judges interpret and apply the national laws in a way that neither protects nor promotes the rights of the weak and the poor and other marginalised parties in the nation. Also, the way they do them in a way violates the peaceful atmosphere of the nation as they seek to help realize the interests of a few. One such example is when certain foreign companies influence the bending of the law to permit them to dump some chemical wastes in certain land without regard for the harmful consequences such graceless decisions will have on the entire nation.

So it is imperative that the judiciary should exercise its interpretation and application of the state laws within and beyond the national boundaries in the light of God's grace if the nationals are to own the government as theirs to protect and provide them with their requirements. Even God in applying his divine justice to His people always does it in the light of his grace—He always carries out His justice in the light of His love. Therefore, it is incumbent on the whole of the judicial system to swim in the ocean of the divine grace.

But how can our national judiciaries deliver acceptable legal services when they are manned by immoral and graceless judges who have been put there by some selfish leaders in the executive and the legislature to meet their narrow interests? If we seriously want to have credible and moral judicial systems in our nations, both the executive and the legislature must desist from putting their personal goals above the national goals. This selfless spirit will assist them appoint some morally dignified men and women to take control of the judiciary as graceful judges with the common good of their people at heart.

God requires all the judicial officials to uphold well His divine grace as the basis of their moral character. If gracious men and women preside over the courts, then the grace of God will automatically permeate the entire judiciary, making it as an oasis of the divine grace. While interpreting and applying the state statutes, the officials should deal with the members of the public not on the basis of their position in society but on the basis of their needs. Courts officials should display their own goodness and generosity as they deal with their fellow human beings.

One of the benefits of a gracious judiciary in the eyes of the general public and in the eyes of God is that the judicial system makes sure that the cost of services in the courts is within the reach of the average citizen. The wise one commands: "Do not exploit the poor because they are poor and do not crush the needy in court, for the Lord will take up their case and will plunder those who plunder them" (Prov. 22:22-23).

Good governance in the judiciary increases when divine

grace is the concrete mark of the ethical values of men and women manning the judicial system. After all, the presence of graciousness in the judiciary is one of the sure indications that divine love is a strong pillar in the judicial system. Otherwise, it would be totally naïve for anyone to talk of good governance in the judiciary and beyond if all the relevant officials lack the essence of divine grace in their moral character. This is so because one of the vital dimensions of divine love is grace. Let our courts have men and women who are full of God's grace to interpret and apply national laws graciously for the common good of mankind.

Nevertheless, without viewing the whole judicial system once more in the clear light of mercy, the third dimension of God's love, we cannot talk of complete good governance in the judiciary. Hence, the primary purpose of the following discussion is to examine ways and means by which good governance can be achieved in the judiciary in the light of God's mercy.

Mercy

Very often, prisoners languish in jails worldwide, denied justice. The majority poor, particularly, have little or no access at all to justice in their nations. And this leads to the fact that small state prisons are filthy, packed with hapless people who have been waiting for justice for ages. Some end their days in these squalid conditions just because some callous law enforcement agent did not see them as worth any attention. Generally, miscarriage of justice is on an alarming increase in many nations, particularly in the Third World countries. People's pathetic conditions echo the words of Christ: they are helpless, like sheep without a shepherd (Matt. 9:36).

Do you see some similarity between the way we treat our

people and the way the Egyptians treated the Israelites as recorded in the Book of Exodus? And would we want God to come down and destroy us like the stonehearted Pharaoh as He gives these people justice? Isn't it better for our judicial systems and other law-enforcing agents to learn to deal mercifully with their fellow human beings for the benefit of mankind? People everywhere badly need the protection of the judiciary, the institution that is mandated to interpret and apply national statutes.

How would you feel if while fleeing from a hungry lion you landed on a venomous snake? Wouldn't you wish you found yourself in the formidable and merciful hands of one who is willing to rescue and protect you? Jesus Christ rebuked and scorned the teachers of the law and the Pharisees for being more concerned with some minute aspects of the Law while neglecting the more important matters such as justice, mercy and faithfulness (Matt.23:23). Judges ought to show mercy and be more concerned with the plight of the people. But this cannot occur unless judiciaries are staffed carefully with men and women who have clothed themselves with the right moral values, especially God's mercy. When the lives of senior judges are guided by God's mercy, the judicial system will start to be influenced by these noble principles.

As the judiciary administers justice to the people, it should do so in the light of God's mercy because a merciful person easily empathises with the needs of others. One of the ways by which the judiciary can show it has embraced God's mercy is by making sure that the cost of the services of the courts is within the means of the average citizen. We ought to be people who empathise with others, since this is how our God is, who when He saw how the Children of Israel were suffering in Egypt said, "I have indeed seen the misery of my people in Egypt. I have heard them crying out because of their slave drivers, and

I am concerned about their suffering. So I have come down to rescue them from the hand of the Egyptians..." (Exod. 3:7-8). We should desist oppressing others, remembering that "It is a dreadful thing to fall into the hands of the living God" (Heb. 10:31).

In order for good governance to prevail within and beyond the four corners of the judiciary, all the court officials should embrace divine mercy as the primary guide for their moral character. It should be the one by which they interpret and apply the state laws as they address the issues of the citizens. Over time, the merciful character of the court judges will automatically permeate the entire judicial systems, making it as the salt and the light of the whole government. And this desirable character could influence other countries as well. It is common knowledge that God and the world seriously want merciful court officials so as to meet the legal needs and the aspirations of the people, especially the miserable and the needy ones.

But we cannot comfortably speak of good governance that is guided by God's love in the judiciary in the absence of persistence, the last dimension of the divine love. So in the following section, we examine the desirable influence in the judiciary of persisting in doing right.

Persistence

"And we urge you, brothers, warn those who are idle, encourage the timid, help the weak, be patient with everyone. Make sure that nobody pays back wrong for wrong, but always try to be kind to each other and to everyone else" (1 Thes. 5:14-15). In this turbulent world of ours where social unrest, unremitting economic and political crises, rampant crimes, family instability, backsliding from the faith and natural disasters have become normal occurrences, our courts and the judges who man them have increased responsibility of patiently handling the issues that come before them so as to keep things moving. Driven by the divine love of God, they should persistently keep warning the idlers to work and earn something for their own living, encourage the timid to press for their rights, particularly in the courts, assist the weak to access justice, prevent people legally not to hurt each other by showing the actual spirit of the law among the nationals, and teach people to be kind to each other.

As we all know, the interpretation and application of the state statutes should be in line with the general welfare of the entire public, and this should be done not only by intelligent judges but also court officials who show extra care and divine persistence. This is because if the courts do not persist in doing things in the right way, consequences will be disastrous for those concerned as well as for the entire nation.

But in order for us to see good judges who persist in interpreting and applying our national laws in the right way, both the executive and the legislature must appoint men and women who are known for being ethical to take charge of the judicial matters. In fact, honest interpretation and application of the law is only possible if done by those whose lives and moral character are guided by divine persistence.

Court judges must therefore, embrace godly persistence as a benchmark for their moral character as well as the standard for guiding the way they do their work. They are to imitate God as their role model in the way He carries out His judgements. For instance, as a Judge, God's persistence in faithfulness was evident in His dealings with the Jews. Although they continually rebelled against Him in the desert, questioning the leadership of Moses, going after idols and wanting to return to Egypt, the patient God did not abandon the Israelites completely.

And God would want the members of the judiciary to emulate His moral characteristics by exercising patience as they deal with their people for the common good of their fellow human beings. They should give themselves sufficient time to examine legal cases thoroughly so that they can reach informed and just verdict.

In conclusion, may I say that in order for good governance to abound in the judiciary in the light of godly persistence, all men and women working in the judicial systems must fully uphold the divine persistence as the guide for their ethical values and as a yardstick for controlling their daily activities. As they interpret and apply the national laws among members of the public, the judicial officials should act patiently, seeing their clients in the light of divine love.

Summary

As I conclude, in order for good governance to exist within and outside the four corners of the judiciary, the entire judicial machinery must sincerely embrace the spirit of God's holiness, righteousness, justice, genuineness, veracity, faithfulness, benevolence, grace, mercy and persistence as the core foundation upon which their moral character, policies and entire operations are based. Failure to this, moral decay and its undesirable consequences will remain in and outside the judicial system. This is sure to happen even if there are some good rules and regulations crafted to fight against the chronic corruption and other social ills. Incarceration may kill but cannot tame a crooked man. The only solution to this old moral problem squarely lies with the moral God who has the ability to not only change a person but also provide for his individual wishes or desires.

General Conclusion

Good governance is only possible in the government when all the activities of the three branches—the executive, the legislature and the judiciary—are conducted in the light of God's moral purity whose elements include holiness, righteousness and justice. Also, in order for the kind of governance that is supported by the Bible to abound, all the three branches of government should carry out their day-to-day tasks in the light of the three aspects of integrity—genuineness, veracity and faithfulness. Good governance also requires that all the three branches of the government embrace and base their daily activities on all the four elements of God's love—benevolence, grace, mercy and persistence. In short, good governance from a biblical perspective is only possible when all the three branches of the government adopt the goodness of God as the guide for their policies and general operations. Really, good governance is the fruit of divine moral qualities.

If we carefully choose people of good character and assign them key duties in the executive, in the legislature and in the judiciary, people whose character is guided by moral purity, integrity and love, we will definitely experience good governance in the different parts of our government. But if we give such significant national tasks to men and women who are morally corrupt, we will not be justified to blame them for not not being agents of good governance in the different systems of our government. It would be strange if we put morally corrupt people in key places and expect them to do right. After all, people reap nothing apart from what they sow.

With the restoration of his lost moral qualities, man automatically starts to practise good governance. Moral purity, integrity and love are the three cornerstones that produce true goodness, leading to good governance. For any human system to experience good governance, man should emulate God in His leadership. So, let man retrace his steps to where he lost his moral values, and he will have recovered his moral qualities. Read this book, act on the truths it communicates, and these truths will change you and help you change your surroundings!

Exercises

1. What does the religion you associate with—Christianity, Islam, Communism, Buddhism, Atheism, etc.—regard as good moral values? How do they impact on good governance and on your personal life and your work? Do they promote or erode the spirit of humanity? If so, how?

2. In what ways can adherence to the biblical Ten Commandments (Exod. 20:1-17) improve man's quality of life and his relationship with God, his Creator?

3. All the ten dimensions of the three elements of moral quality (moral purity, integrity, love) are key pillars of good governance and brotherly relationships. Discuss.

4. If people working in the government were to be morally upright, accordingly, the government will be morally upright. Conversely, a bad and corrupt government is the product of bad and corrupt people. Explain.

5. Corruption involves human thought, word and action. Explain.

Bibliography

Douglas, J. D, ed. New Bible Dictionary. Wheaton, Illinois: Tyndale House Publishers, 1988.

Erickson, Milliard J. Christian Theology, Unabridged, One-Volume Edition. Grand Rapids, Michigan: Baker Book House, 1996.

Kriegbaum, Richard. Leadership Prayers. Wheaton, Illinois: Tyndale House Publishers, INC., 1998.

Berkley, James D., ed. Leadership Handbook of Management and Administration: Practical insight from a cross section of ministry leaders. Grand Rapids, Michigan: Baker Books, 2000.

MacArthur, John. The Master's Plan for the Church. Chicago: Moody Press, 1991.

T., Henry, and Richard Blackaby. Spiritual Leadership: The Interactive Study. Nashville, Tennessee: Broadman and Holman Publishers, 2006.

Nwabuzor, E, and M. Mueller. An Introduction to Political Science for African Students. Hong Kong: The Macmillan Press Ltd., 1993.